"Recalling the miracle of the six ~~jars~~ ~~turned into choice~~ wine at Cana, Teri and John Bosio provide a hands-on reflection for every married couple. Grounded on the awareness that the grace of Christ empowers married couples, *Six Jars of Love* explores six keys to enrich marital love on the journey of life. This book also could serve as a wonderful guide for groups of couples seeking to enrich their marriage."

ARCHBISHOP JOSEPH KURTZ, *Archdiocese of Louisville*

"*Six Jars of Love* invites Catholic couples to recognize the presence of Mary and Jesus in their marriage ready to help them as they helped the couple at the wedding at Cana. The book is an invitation for spouses to pray and grow in love following Jesus' example—a useful reading for all couples to enjoy together."

BISHOP J. MARK SPALDING, *Diocese of Nashville*

"John and Teri Bosio's *Six Jars of Love* will lead you to visit places where you are, or have been, as a couple. At the end, you will be deeply spiritually transformed. We really like *Six Jars of Love*, it's a great roadmap for all married couples."

CHRISTIAN AND CHRISTINE MEERT, *founders of Agape CatholicMarriagePrep.com*

"If you want a happy marriage than you want a holy marriage. Read this book with your spouse, and then read it again!"

JON LEONETTI, *Catholic speaker and best-selling author*

"*Six Jars of Love* is a great concept for a book on marriage. It's an image that really worked for us. Stories are such a rich and powerful way to transmit information! This book is full of them. The chapter devoted to generosity in marriage is especially good. Not many books on marriage devote themselves to this topic. This book will be a very welcome addition among the tools any Catholic couple would want to have in their toolbox."

STEVE AND KATHY BEIRNE, *authors of the Foundations Newsletter for Newly Married Couples*

"I LOVED this work! The overall approach is so reader friendly and powerfully effective! The language is real and always relatable to anyone and the format is such that it flows smoothly paging through the work to find what grabs you, or to read it straight through without tiring. Bravo for sure!"

DEACON STEPHEN BOWLING, *Family Life Director, Archdiocese of Louisville*

"*Six Jars of Love* is an incredibly easy-to-read and understand book for couples, and all those who work with couples. The six loving attitudes detailed within, capture the essence of how a couple's life can manifest God's love in the world. I am definitely adding this jewel to our must-read recommendations for the engaged couples, too."

SOCORRO TRUCHAN, *Associate Director, Secretariat for Parish Life & Lay Leadership, Domestic Church, Catholic Diocese of Kalamazoo*

SIX JARS OF LOVE

LOVING ATTITUDES TO HELP MARRIED COUPLES RECONNECT

JOHN AND TERI BOSIO

TWENTY-THIRD
PUBLICATIONS
twentythirdpublications.com

IMPRIMATUR
+Most Rev. J. Mark Spalding, DD, JCL
Bishop of Nashville
Diocese of Nashville
23 January 2019

NIHIL OBSTAT
Rev. Andrew J. Bulso, STL
Censor Librorum

Twenty-Third Publications
One Montauk Avenue, Suite 200
New London, CT 06320
(860) 437-3012 or (800) 321-0411
www.twentythirdpublications.com

Copyright © 2019 John and Teri Bosio. All rights reserved. No part of this publication may be reproduced in any manner without prior written permission of the publisher. Write to the Permissions Editor.

Cover photo: iStockphoto.com / SimonSkafar

ISBN: 978-1-62785-463-4
Library of Congress Control Number: 2019940114
Printed in the U.S.A.

A division of Bayard, Inc.

Contents

Introduction

DURING THE YEARS OF MY PRACTICE AS A MARRIAGE AND FAMILY THERAPIST, I (JOHN) MET MANY COUPLES WHO CAME TO ME COMPLAINING THAT THEY WERE GROWING DISTANT—DRIFTING APART. One couple in particular stands out as a typical example. Jim and Mary had been married seven years and were parents of two very active toddlers. They were also both working full time.

As they sat in my office I could tell that they were tired, stressed, and angry at each other. Mary felt overwhelmed, and Jim was bitter because he felt ignored by his wife and did not want to be in my office.

Mary complained: "Many evenings, after spending eight hours at work, I find myself coming home to cook dinner, fold the laundry, and play with our sons, Jack and Mike, or give them a bath and put them to bed. Meanwhile, Jim is either in the garage working on his favorite hobby, his car, or playing video games."

Turning toward Jim, she said: "What about me? When do I get a break? I'm exhausted!"

Mary paused for a few seconds to compose herself and then continued: "I often wonder what's happened to us. We still have the wedding pictures on our coffee table, yet we feel miles apart. How did we end up feeling so distant?"

Mary and Jim were suffering because they were mourning the intimate connection they once had with each other. They could still remember their wedding day very vividly, but the warmth of their relationship was slowly fading. They seldom saw smiles on each other's faces. All they felt was pain, frustration, and anger, and they could not give each other comfort. They felt lonely, and they were thinking: Is this all there is?

Jim and Mary are a normal couple. What they were facing was a crisis in their relationship—a crisis that is common to most spouses. Dr. William Doherty, a sociologist at the University of Minnesota and a marriage therapist, compares what happens to couples after they marry to what happens to someone who sets out on a voyage on the Mississippi River with a canoe. No matter how much love the spouses feel for each other, writes Dr. Doherty, if they do not intentionally paddle together to stay on course, they tend to drift apart emotionally. Life's river currents take them to places that they did not plan to visit, far away from their intended destination.

In *Take Back Your Marriage*,[1] Dr. Doherty explains that this drifting is something that all couples experience throughout their lives. We are all prone to becoming complacent in our relationship, and we tend to take each other for granted. We let our relationship go on autopilot and don't realize that we are slowly growing distant.

We asked couples we know in our community: How do you know when you are drifting? These are couples in stable marriages who were willing to share their journey with us. Here is what they said:

Bill I know we are drifting when I feel something is missing—like I'm missing my best friend.

Beth We have many little squabbles—nothing serious. We are short with each other for no special reason.

Mark When we find that we don't have anything to talk about, it tells me we are drifting.

Barb I think we're drifting when I catch myself thinking: It doesn't matter what he wants to do; I'm doing what I want.

Gina When Bob went back to school, it was a difficult time. That commitment took over a large part of our free time to be together.

Bob (agrees) Yes, I was very busy, and I felt isolated, and we disconnected.

The problem for most couples is that growing distant is so gradual that, unless we are aware of the possibility and are watchful, it is difficult to know that we are drifting apart. We may feel some discomfort, but we ignore it. We blame our busy schedules or our spouse. We feel the pain, and we carry on. We dive deeper into our work, or we turn our attention to the needs of our children, or distract ourselves with sports, hobbies, or friends on social media, or we busy ourselves with volunteer work, even church work. It is only after months or years that we realize that we are not where we want to be. We are becoming emotionally disconnected. We do not know each other anymore. Our lives are moving on different tracks, in different directions.

Have you ever felt that you were drifting? How would you recognize that you are drifting? How do you reconnect?

Unfortunately there are some couples whose canoe is so far off course that they cannot find their way back. They do not think they have the energy to rebuild their relationship. Too much damage has been done. Some jump ship; others settle in an uncomfortable marriage, not knowing what to do. However, it does not have to be this way. Fortunately there are many more couples that, inspired by their faith and by what they believe about marriage, seek the help and guidance of a good book, or a couples' retreat, or the advice of a priest or a professional marriage therapist. Be one of these!

Pope Francis' Advice to Jim and Mary and to Us

In his apostolic exhortation *The Joy of Love* (*Amoris Laetitia*) Pope Francis, as a caring pastor, gives couples like Jim and Mary, whom we met at the beginning of this book, and to all of us some helpful marriage advice. Here are some of his thoughts.

- Married life is a long journey and with the help of God's grace, you make progress by working on it one day at a time (n. 218).

- Remember that neither one of you is perfect, and each must set aside all illusions and accept the other as he or she actually is: a work in progress (n. 218).

- Married life is a process of growth, and each of you is an instrument through which God helps the other mature. "The greatest mission of two people in love is to help one another become, respectively, more a man and more a woman" (n. 221).

- Hope is what helps you make progress on your journey together. Hope is the leaven that makes it possible for you to look beyond the present conflicts and arguments and see your current situation in a broader perspective (n. 219).

- Generosity and sacrifice are required throughout your marriage. At each stage of your life you need to sit down and renegotiate your agreements so that there are no winners and losers (n. 220).

- Learn to be present to each other. Make time for each other. Develop daily rituals, such as a morning kiss, an evening blessing, waiting at the door to welcome each other home, taking trips together, and sharing household chores; and it helps to break the routine with an occasional party (n. 225).

- Remember that "none of this is possible without praying to the Holy Spirit for an outpouring of his grace" (n. 164).

- "Love is always a gift from God" (n. 228).

These are great words of advice! Pope Francis writes that our hopes for the future give us a special motivation. Hope gives us a vision of what can be. It compels us to take control of our canoe and reset the direction of our journey. We believe that this hope and motivation come from something deep in our heart; they come from the meaning we give to our voyage—the reason we got into the canoe.

"In the strongest marriages, husband and wife share a deep sense of meaning." ▪ **DR. JOHN GOTTMAN, PHD**[2]

The Importance of Meaning

In order for couples to find the interior strength and energy to stay on course and to build their marriage, they need to be convinced that what they are doing is worthwhile and has a purpose—a meaning that is compelling. This is what gives them the hope and the courage to persist and to make the necessary adjustments and even sacrifices.

That day in my office, I asked Jim and Mary many questions: "Why did you get married? What were your dreams for your life? Are they still the same today? What do you want for your future?" I was trying to help them find in their heart the reason—the meaning—for being together that would give them the hope and the strength to make the changes they needed to reconnect.

Viktor Frankl, an Austrian psychiatrist and a Holocaust survivor, wrote in *Man's Search for Meaning* about the importance of finding a purpose, a meaning. He writes that the meaning of life can be found in every moment of our life; even in suffering and death. This is what he learned while imprisoned at the Auschwitz concentration camp. He writes that those who found meaning in their life found the strength to endure and, for some, even to survive.

John Gottman, a psychologist who studied married couples extensively, wrote in *The Seven Principles for Making Marriage Work* that one of these principles is "shared meaning." To be happy, spouses need to find a common reason for their relationship, one that transcends them, something that propels them forward on their voyage together and guides them when they get lost. Marriage is not just about sharing a home and raising kids. It is about something more. It is the pursuit of a vision of life that guides the spouses to build a life together, a life that has a purpose.

For Christian couples the meaning for their life together comes from their faith. In my conversation with Jim and Mary I heard them say: "We got married in the Church because we thought it would mean something to us. Right now, we do not know exactly what that is, except that we know God is with us."

The sense that God is present in one's marriage is a particularly powerful predictor of marital success among young married parents in America today. ■ **THE STATE OF OUR UNIONS, 2011**[3]

The Power of Faith

Couples married in the Church face the same challenging passages and difficulties as all other couples. What is different for them is the presence in their life of a light that shines on their path and shows them the way in the face of obstacles. Pope Francis explains that we can see the beauty and attractiveness of marriage and family life when they are anchored in the love of God.[4] Our Catholic faith gives us a very clear map and compass for our canoe voyage and disposes us to receive the graces we need to overcome the obstacles we encounter. Our Christian faith helps us see that our marriage is not about us; it is a calling from God to serve him by being married, raising a family, and contributing to society. This calling gives meaning to our life.

On our wedding day, as baptized persons, we accepted a mission from God: to be icons of his love in our communities. We gave ourselves to each other completely and brought Christ with us in our canoe. Today, Christ is in our home; he is paddling our canoe with us and giving us the graces we need to steer our marriage in the right direction. With him as our companion, we let God chart our course and write our story.

"This is holiness: to let God write our history."
■ **POPE FRANCIS**[5]

This Book: Six Jars of Love

The goal of this book is to help you be aware of Christ's presence in your canoe and to let him guide you and help you steer your vessel in the right direction.

Six Jars of Love is a book to be savored. Read it at your own pace. The chapters that follow were developed from presentations that we give at couples' retreats for parishes and dioceses. You can read this book with other couples and support each other as you grow in your marriages. Or you can read it together with your spouse as a private spiritual retreat at home.

We want to stress that while it is best if you and your spouse read these chapters together, it is not necessary. If you read this book on your own, know that any improvement in attitude that one of you makes is bound to invite the other to respond in kind. Just as a negative interaction elicits a negative response, a positive one invites a positive response.

We suggest that you read a chapter at a time, and then for a few days pray and reflect on what you read, and practice what you learned. Let God's grace prepare your heart while you give the message of each chapter time to sink in, ferment, and make a difference in your life. Let it affect the behaviors and rituals through which you interact with your spouse and with your children. Create new habits—positive habits. Most of all, during this time, remember that Jesus is with you in your canoe. Pray for your marriage and for your spouse, and practice your faith. Scientists at the National Marriage Project[6] are finding that the practice of one's faith and the involvement in one's community are two important predictors of marital success.

As you read and reflect on the chapters of this book, make a commitment to attend Sunday Mass together regularly. When you participate in the Mass you bring your marriage to the Trinity, Father, Son, and Holy Spirit, who are present on the altar and in the assembly. In the Eucharist you encounter Jesus; you hear his word, eat his Body, and receive from him the graces you need to let love grow in your relationship. Pope Francis told his audience on December 13, 2017[7] that it is at Mass that we find our strength. He added that without the gift of the Eucharist we "are condemned to be dominated by the fatigue of everyday life." This fatigue is what causes our marriage canoe to drift and go off course. The Eucharist can help you stay on track.

In addition, consider attending the social activities of your parish and meeting other couples; and if your time permits, volunteer to serve. Making friends with people who have similar values can be of great support to your marriage. Marriages do not grow in isolation.

We hope that through your prayers and through this book, you become more aware of Christ's presence in your life and you are able to keep your canoe on the right course. Let God write your story. As you do, you will become an icon of God's love, and you and your spouse will experience in your relationship the joy of love. This is God's dream for you.[8]

---

*"Christian spouses can make their marriage
a journey to holiness."* ■ **BENEDICT XVI OCTOBER 27, 2010**

PRAYER

It was because of Mary's intervention that, at the wedding at Cana, Jesus changed six jars of water into exquisite wine and helped a newly married couple avoid a terrible embarrassment. Mary and Jesus are great companions to have in your marriage. Through Mary you can ask Jesus to guide you and give you the graces you need as you progress on your journey.

At the end of each chapter we will ask you to pray the Hail Mary, the Memorare, which is a centuries-old Catholic prayer, and the Glory Be.

Hail Mary

Hail Mary, full of grace,
the Lord is with you;
blessed are you among women,
and blessed is the fruit of your womb, Jesus.
Holy Mary, Mother of God,
pray for us sinners
now and at the hour of our death,
Amen.

Memorare

Remember, O most gracious Virgin Mary,
that never was it known
that anyone who fled to your protection,
implored your help or sought your intercession
was left unaided.
Inspired by this confidence,
we fly unto you, O Virgin of Virgins our mother;
to you do we come, before you we stand,
sinful and sorrowful;
O Mother of the Word Incarnate,
despise not our petitions,
but in your mercy hear and answer us.
Amen.

Glory Be

Glory be to the Father, and to the Son, and to the Holy Spirit;
as it was in the beginning, is now and ever shall be,
world without end.
Amen.

PERSONAL/COUPLE REFLECTION

1. How is your marriage voyage progressing? Is your canoe moving in the right direction or is it drifting off course?

2. What are some of the currents that are pulling your canoe off course?

3. Pope Francis writes that hope is the source of strength in marriage. What are your hopes and dreams for your life?

4. What is your purpose as a couple—what gives meaning to your marriage?

5. Looking back, what led you to take this voyage together?

6. How do you practice your faith? What role does faith play in your marriage?

GROUP SHARING

1. Based on your experience of marriage, is the metaphor of the canoe appropriate? Why?

2. What are the currents today that steer marriages away from their intended destination?

3. In your opinion, what is the destination?

4. Why is meaning important in life?

5. What are some of the red flags that tell couples they are going off course?

6. Do you agree that faith practice and community involvement are important? Why or why not?

Chapter 1

The Wedding at Cana

IN 2012 WE ATTENDED THE SEVENTH WORLD MEETING OF FAMILIES, HELD IN MILAN, ITALY. Pope Benedict XVI was present, and he spoke to the thousands of people who had gathered. A young couple from Madagascar asked the pontiff for his grandfatherly advice about getting married. He replied by first affirming their feelings of love for each other. He said: "Falling in love is a wonderful thing," and the crowd responded with thundering applause. Then, the pope added that feelings do not last forever. These loving sentiments will fade and for love to last it needs to become a conscious decision. What happens in all marriages is like what happened at the wedding of Cana, the Pope said: "The first wine is very fine: this is falling in love. But those feelings do not last until the end: a second wine has to come later, it has to ferment and grow, to mature…This 'second wine' is more wonderful still, it is better than the first wine."

The wedding at Cana is a significant point of reference in our Catholic tradition. It reminds us of the goodness of marriage and the role that Jesus and Mary can play in the life of married couples.

Do you remember what happened at Cana? Below is the passage from the Gospel of John that describes the event. Read it slowly. Listen to each word, imagining that you are there.

The Wedding at Cana (*John 2:1–11*)

On the third day there was a wedding in Cana in Galilee, and the mother of Jesus was there. Jesus and his disciples were also invited to the wedding. When the wine ran short, the mother of Jesus said to him, "They have no wine." [And] Jesus said to her, "Woman, how does your concern affect me? My hour has not yet come." His mother said to the servers, "Do whatever he tells you." Now there were six stone water jars there for Jewish ceremonial washings, each holding twenty to thirty gallons. Jesus told them, "Fill the jars with water." So they filled them to the brim. Then he told them, "Draw some out now and take it to the headwaiter." So they took it. And when the headwaiter tasted the water that had become wine, without knowing where it came from (although the servers who had drawn the water knew), the headwaiter called the bridegroom and said to him, "Everyone serves good wine first, and then when people have drunk freely, an inferior one; but you have kept the good wine until now." Jesus did this as the beginning of his signs in Cana in Galilee and so revealed his glory, and his disciples began to believe in him.

A Disaster Avoided

This is the story of a wedding disaster that was avoided thanks to the kindness of two guests. Wine was a beverage that was expected in abundance at a wedding. Had the feast run out of wine, the couple and the family would have faced a major embarrassment in their town. What saved their special day was the presence of Mary and Jesus and their intervention. They stepped forward to make up for the couple's shortcoming, and Jesus turned six large jars of water into exquisite wine. That was quite a wedding gift.

This is the story of any marriage: of yours and ours. We all have shortcomings that cause our wine to run short from time to time, and this happens at all stages of marriage. In fact, even after forty-six years we continue to encounter moments that cause stress to our relationship.

It happened as I was planning to retire. Teri would justifiably ask: "What are you going to do when you retire?" I did not understand the significance of her question. "It is retirement; I do not want to plan what I am going to do. I may go for walks, take pictures, go on trips, etc." Teri would reply with another fair question: "What will I do while you do that?" She was concerned about how this might impact her and change her routine. Instead, I resented her questions. I misunderstood her intentions. These exchanges caused tension in our relationship, and at a time when we should have been rejoicing, we were anxious because we were getting on each other's nerves.

If you are a normal couple, you have certainly found yourself in situations that have taken the joy out of your relationship. For example, there may have been times when you experienced rejection from your spouse instead of acceptance. You felt ignored or lied to instead of being given the attention you wanted or the honesty you deserved. You may have suffered because of your spouse's selfish acts, or you may have found it difficult to forgive and carried the burden of your resentment for too long. You may have felt alone in moments of pain when your spouse was not there to help you. Many of these difficulties were caused unintentionally, but others came out of selfishness. If you are suffering right now because of similar or other stressors in your relationship, resolve to ask Mary and Jesus to help you, like they helped the couple at Cana.

Running Out of Wine Is Natural

Brent and Tina are good friends of ours, whom we have known for many years. They told us about an event that caused them a lot of pain. Brent and Tina were both missing their families and their hometown, which was several states away, and they had talked about moving back, but no decision had been made. One day, Brent came home and announced boldly: "We are going to move back home and I have already told my family in our hometown." This took Tina by surprise. "What about me? Don't I count? Why did you decide to tell your family before you told me?" This caused a deep wound. I am certain you understand why. This was a moment in their marriage when they were not on the same page. Tina was hurt.

Dr. John Gottman, a researcher who studied married couples for over forty years, writes that the brain is wired to remember bad things more than good ones and it takes five positive interactions to offset the damage done by a bad one.

In the story of Brent and Tina, one thoughtless action created a lot of pain and required much positive care over time to heal the wound. Several negative exchanges in a short time can cause our emotional bank account to quickly run in the red. Gottman advises couples to store up good feelings for each other so that when something negative happens it will take less effort to undo the damage.

Think about your own life experiences. How long does it take for you and your spouse to recover from a negative exchange that has caused hurt feelings? For us, depending on the level of hurt, it takes time, a lot of small favors, gentle words, and intentional positive behaviors to reset the course of our relationship. Think about the state of your emotional bank account. Do you, right now, have a surplus of good feelings toward your spouse? Or is your balance running so low that anything negative, even small, can put you in a state of deficit?

How Do We Build Up a Surplus of Good Wine?

Years ago, when I (John) was a practicing marriage therapist, couples came to my office asking for help. These were couples that realized they were running out of wine. As the therapist I felt like one of the servers at the wedding at Cana. My job was to help these hurting couples fill their empty jars, and like the waiters at Cana all I had to offer them was water.

I could not give them the second wine—the good wine that their hearts desired. The second wine requires a miracle: it requires Jesus' presence. Pope Francis tells us: "Love is a gift of God" (*Amoris Laetitia* [AL], 228). What all couples really want deep down is "supernatural love." They long to taste of the goodness of God in the love of one's beloved. But that love is not something we can create for ourselves. It requires God's grace. We need to let the Holy Spirit transform our life and our love. The Catechism reminds us that Christ gives us "the strength… to love one another with supernatural, tender and fruitful love" (*Catechism of the Catholic Church* [CCC], 1642). This is the exquisite wine we all desire.

To help my clients experience the taste of true love, I would teach them the skills they needed for getting along—that was the water for their jars. At the same time, I would encourage them to invite Jesus and Mary into their marriage to help them turn their water into exquisite wine. Only through Jesus and through the power of the Holy Spirit can we experience the true fruits of supernatural love: *joy*, *peace*, and *mercy*, as we learn from the

Catechism (CCC, 1829). These fruits give us the taste of the good wine that makes our heart smile.

"Do whatever he tells you."

At the wedding at Cana, Mary said to the servers: "Do whatever he tells you." To allow Jesus to turn our water into good wine, we need to do what he tells us. This requires faith. Benedict XVI and Pope Francis teach us that our Christian faith is not an ideology that we embrace; rather, it is an encounter with the person of Jesus who gives our life a new meaning.[9] Faith allows us to see our marriage from God's perspective and to hear what Jesus is telling us. Faith disposes us to let the Holy Spirit transform our attitudes and conform our way of loving to Jesus' way of loving. Faith gives meaning to all aspects of a couple's life: the good times and the tough times. Pope Francis writes that moments of pain will be experienced in union with Christ, and moments of joy will be cherished as a sharing in Christ's resurrection.[10] Faith also gives us the strength to resist the temptations that can destroy our marriage. Bill, a friend of ours, told us: "I travel a tremendous amount of time, and one thing that I do is to try to stay out of bars. I try to stay out of situations that can create temptations for me. And there are times when I turn to God and say: 'Please help me because I cannot do it by myself!'"

Benedict XVI stressed the importance of faith in his homily at the opening of the Synod on Faith in 2012: "There is a clear link between the crisis in faith and the crisis in marriage."[11] Social scientists agree with the pontiff. Researchers are finding that couples who practice their faith are less likely to have affairs or to divorce. Faith increases the chances that a couple will be happy.[12] In 2011 the National Marriage Project conducted a study about the marital satisfaction of parents. They wrote: "couples who regularly attend a church, synagogue, or mosque together enjoy higher levels of marital success." And they explained that a key factor in a couple's success is their belief that God is present in their marriage.[13]

Jesus and Mary Are Present in Your Daily Life

Do you know that during the good times and the difficult times, Jesus and Mary are present in your life even if you are not aware of them? On your wedding day you invited them to be with you on your journey, and they have come. Therefore, when you are stressed or encounter a conflict with your spouse, turn to them with confidence and ask for their help and guidance. You will not be disappointed. St. John Paul II said: "Jesus does not stand by and leave you alone to face the challenge. He is always with you to transform your weakness into strength."[14] Mary and Jesus are ready to help you no matter the situation, even when you hit rock bottom.

Jerry is a joyful gentleman in his eighties. One day, as Teri and I were leaving church, he told us that he was celebrating a special anniversary. It was his thirty-fifth anniversary of sobriety. His wife had died recently, and she was very much on his mind because she helped him save their marriage. It was because of her and God's grace that he was able to stop drinking. His addiction had become so bad that he would have blackouts and car accidents. One day his wife, Marilyn, told him: "You have to make a choice. It is either the bottle or me. What will it be?" He chose Marilyn and gave up the bottle. He added that he could not have done it without the help of God's grace and the intercession of St. Jude.

At Cana, Jesus gave the newlywed couple not just the wine they needed to satisfy the immediate thirst of their guests, but the very best wine—a wine to be proud of, a wine the guests remembered and probably talked about for some time after the wedding.

"The alliance of love between a man and a woman, an alliance for life, cannot be improvised, and is not made in a day."
▨ **POPE FRANCIS**[15]

The Six Jars

The gospel story of the wedding at Cana mentions that there were six jars in the banquet room. We believe that each marriage has six jars, which with the help of Mary and Jesus can be filled with the good wine. We call these jars the "six jars of love."

Each of these jars represents a key attitude without which a couple's love cannot grow. In fact, without them it dies. Attitudes are mental stances we take toward another person. These attitudes affect the way we behave toward our spouse. Attitudes shape our habits.

"Attitude is a little thing that makes a big difference."
▨ **WINSTON CHURCHILL**

Attitudes

Researchers are finding that between forty and forty-five percent of our daily interactions are driven by our habits, and our habits are shaped by our attitudes. One of John's colleagues shared the following anecdote to illustrate how her attitude toward her husband was affecting a habit that was damaging their relationship. "The other day," she said, "my husband wanted to make sure I answered his call so he borrowed my son Ed's cell phone to call me. As I answered I was surprised to hear my husband's voice, but I was most surprised by his explanation. He said: 'I used Ed's phone because I wanted to hear your "caring" voice. I don't get this "kind" tone when you know that I'm calling.' Then, he said: 'this kind and caring voice is normally reserved only for Ed and our dog.'"

"This incident and his comments," continued the young mother, "left me feeling disturbed. The more I thought about it, the more I realized that he had a point. My poor attitude toward my husband leads me to express more care and affection to the dog and to our fourteen-year-old son."

"At dinner that evening," she continued, "we discussed the incident, and we admitted that we both could do better with our attitudes toward each other. We agreed to express our care and affection for each other more often. I said to my husband jokingly: 'I promise that if you spend as much time with me as you spend with the dog, and if you pet me like you pet the dog, my voice will sound more caring and kind to you.' We both laughed, understanding that in all of this there was a lesson to be learned."

Our attitudes shape our behaviors, which when repeated become habits.

Attitudes That Express Love

The six jars of love contain six attitudes that express love: *Welcome*, *Faithfulness*, *Generosity*, *Forgiveness*, *Compassion*, and *Service*.

In my research, I (John) found that most psychologists and scholars link the presence of these attitudes to the stability of a marriage relationship and to the happiness of a couple. They all admit that the absence of even just one of these undermines the marriage and leads couples to feeling miserable. These attitudes represent qualities of love that are crucial to your marital success. They help couples develop habits that keep them from drifting apart and stay on course on their journey, such as a good morning and a good night kiss, not interrupting while listening, telling the truth, holding hands, scheduling regular date nights, eating meals together, managing the interruptions from our digital gadgets, attending Mass weekly, asking forgiveness, expressing compassion and empathy, helping each other in our daily chores, remembering to say "please" and "thank you," and many others.

In the coming chapters we will reflect on each of the loving attitudes that help us develop good habits and give us a taste of the love our heart longs for: welcome, faithfulness, generosity, forgiveness, compassion, and service. But first, in Chapter 2 you are invited to celebrate your love story.

Throughout the book we will keep in mind Pope Francis's message that growing in love requires daily effort, and that such growth is not possible without praying to the Holy Spirit to transform our love (AL,164).

PRAYER

Mary and Jesus,
special friends of the couple at Cana
and honored guests in our marriage,
we turn to you.

You helped a couple in their moment of need.
Watch over us and help us
when our wine runs short.

We yearn to fill our marriage with the good wine
that God alone can give.

Help us change our attitudes
and fill our life and our hearts
with a love for each other that reflects imperfectly
the immense love of the Father, the Son and the Holy Spirit.
Amen.

Together recite the Hail Mary, the Memorare, and the Glory Be (these prayers can be found on pages 10–11).

PERSONAL/COUPLE REFLECTION

1. You and your spouse are like the couple at the wedding at Cana. How is your supply of wine holding up? Are your jars full or are you running short?

2. The authors identify six attitudes necessary for a healthy marriage: welcome, faithfulness, generosity, forgiveness, compassion, and service. Which of these do you think is a strength in your marriage, and which is in need of improvement?

3. When and how are you most aware of Mary and Jesus' presence in your life?

4. How do you pray? How are you most comfortable praying?

GROUP SHARING

1. Discuss the importance of the six attitudes identified in this chapter: welcome, faithfulness, generosity, forgiveness, compassion, and service. Can you relate these to your day-to-day life?

2. Why do you think these are important to your marriage relationship? What would a marriage that is missing one of these attitudes feel and look like?

3. We will explain each of these attitudes in the chapters to come. For now reflect on them, drawing from your experience. Consider each of them, and identify words or actions that you think show the presence of these attitudes in a marriage.
   a. Welcome
   b. Faithfulness
   c. Generosity
   d. Forgiveness
   e. Compassion
   f. Service

PRACTICE

During the coming week, pause from time to time and say a short prayer to Mary and Jesus asking for help with a jar that needs to be filled.

Chapter 2

Celebrate Your Love Story

EVERY MARRIAGE IS A LOVE STORY.

Do you remember how your love story started?

When we lead a retreat for couples, from time to time we ask husbands and wives to recall how they met and to share their first impressions of each other. Here are the memories shared by three couples.

First Encounters – First Impressions

George and Mary

George Mary and her mother were staying at the same hotel where I was staying, and they stopped me to ask a question: "Do you know a good place to get something to drink?" As I was giving them directions I was attracted by the color of Mary's hair and the vibrant blue of her eyes—all wrapped in the shyness of her smile. After I was finished giving directions, I winked at Mary. She blushed and smiled at me. That was the beginning.

Mark and Jackie

Mark   I was in the military, and I was home for the holidays, and I was eager to meet someone.

Jackie   Our eyes met at a soda fountain. He followed me next door and stood next to me at a card counter, and said: "Hi, are you looking for a card?" What an original pick-up line!

John and Barb

John   My friend was dating Barb. One day we went on a double date, and when I saw them together I thought to myself: What does he see in her?

Barb   When I saw John with his date and how he was dressed I thought: Wow, white shoes, white pants. Some sort of nerd! Yuck!

John   About a year later I knew she was the person God was sending me.

Do you remember how you and your spouse first met? Can you mentally put yourself there and relive that first encounter? What were your first impressions?

"Falling in love is a wonderful thing."
■ **BENEDICT XVI**

Providence

For most married couples that first encounter was a providential one—a coincidence that changed their life. That was a moment in time, which, had it not happened, the relationship may not have started and your love story may not have existed.

Providence is a word that we find appropriate when we consider all the circumstances, all the coincidences, that brought the two of us together. John was born in northern Italy, and Teri was born in Vermont. We grew up far away from each other and with very different life experiences. A lot had to happen for both of us to move, at about the same time, to Overland Park, Kansas, and join Holy Cross Catholic Church. Couples who look at their love stories through the eyes of faith can see the hand of God's providence guiding them.

Teri My father was in the Air Force, and we moved a lot and lived in many parts of the country, even overseas. When I was a teenager we lived in Bangkok, Thailand. It was there that I experienced the beginning of our love story. At age fourteen I started noticing boys and realized that God was calling me to one day be married. I shared this with a friend, and together we started praying for our future husbands, being quite aware that they were "somewhere" in the world. Each day, during one of our school breaks, we would go to the chapel, kneel in front of an image of Mary, and pray. I often wondered where my future husband was and what he might be doing and continued praying for him through high school and college.

John　Meanwhile, I lived in Italy, where I grew up in a very
tight-knit family. We lived in the same household with
my grandparents, my mother's parents. During my
teenage years I was in the seminary because I thought
I wanted to be a priest. I was preparing to become a
missionary to Africa. As I reached college my religious
community sent me to Washington, DC, to study
theology at the Catholic University of America. There,
I grew less certain about my vocation and asked for a
leave of absence. During my leave, I moved to Kansas
and was hired as the Director of Religious Education
at Church of the Holy Cross in Overland Park. After
a year I knew that the priesthood was not my calling,
and I decided to remain in the United States and
continue working in parish ministry as a layperson.

　　At the same time that I moved to Overland Park,
Teri's family also relocated there, and during the
summer of 1971 Teri worked at Holy Cross as the
parish secretary. It was there, in the parish office, that
I first met Teri. It was through working together on
a variety of projects that I gradually got to know her
and felt an attraction to her. We dated for almost a year
before we became engaged.

It Is in God's Design

St. John Paul II said in 1982, while visiting the shrine of Our
Lady of Fatima, a year after surviving an assassination attempt:
"In the designs of Providence there are no mere coincidences."

　　The hand of God is present in all our love stories, and
what seem to be coincidences are acts of God's providence.

To illustrate this point, I (Teri) often tell the story of how my family started attending Holy Cross parish. When we moved to Overland Park from Chicago, our home was located on the boundaries of three adjacent parishes. After visiting all three, my dad asked us which parish we should join. Ultimately he decided that the family would become members of Holy Cross. He was reluctant to join Holy Cross because the family would have to participate in yet another church building campaign, but he acknowledged that the house was within the boundaries of Holy Cross, even if at the edge. That decision was a providential moment for us. Had my family joined a different parish, John and I may have never met.

Can you think of people or events in your life that were providential to bringing the two of you together to begin your love story?

Name Your Story

We like to talk about love stories because we believe that every marriage is a love story. And, as you know, every love story has its moments of ecstasy, romance, challenging times, sad experiences, and everything in between, just like you find in the stories told in movies or novels today.

During our marriage retreats we often ask couples to pretend that a famous filmmaker has decided to make a movie based on their love story. We ask: "What type (genre) of movie will it be? Will it be: a romance, a drama, a mystery, an action adventure, a comedy, etc.?" Finally we ask couples to name the movie.

We remember vividly the answers given by two couples in particular. One was married about ten years. They titled their love story: "Ode to Joy." They explained that "Ode to Joy" was played at their wedding, and they wanted it to be the theme of their entire marriage. The other couple, Doris and Ken, married almost fifty years, titled their movie: "War and Peace." We asked them to explain the reason for the title. Doris said that early in their marriage they were looking for a way to spend fun time together. They discovered that both loved sailing, so they purchased a small sailboat. They had a lot of fun together sailing on the local lakes. Later, they upgraded the size of their vessel and started racing competitively together. Under the pressure of the competition they found themselves arguing and getting upset with each other. So, they named their boat "War & Peace," and that is what they wanted to name their story.

Now think about your own story.

What type of movie would your story be: a comedy, a drama, a romance?

What title will it have?

It is possible that you and your spouse don't agree on the movie genre or on the title for your story. That is OK. It makes the conversation more interesting.

"All, everything I understand,
I understand only because I love."
■ **LEO TOLSTOY (WAR AND PEACE)**

You Are Not Alone

We find it helpful to think of each marriage as a love story that is guided by God's providence and shaped by the choices the spouses make in response to the events and people God put on their path. God wants to write your story, and holiness is letting him write it, says Pope Francis.[16]

When we think about this, we realize that our story, the John and Teri story, does not stand alone. It is connected to and influenced by the love stories of many other people: our parents and grandparents, our friends, neighbors, priests and nuns, and through this network of relationships we all influence one another. When other couples suffer, we all suffer. Likewise, our happiness affects one another positively.

Your story is connected across generations to the love stories from the past: your parents, your grandparents, great-grandparents, and so on. Your story is also connected to future generations. Through your example you influence the love stories of your children, grandchildren, great grandchildren, and generations to come.

The Family Is the First School on How to Be Human

One day while doing spring cleaning in my filing cabinet, I (John) came across a folder that I had not touched in years. Curious about its content, I opened it and found in it a small treasure. It was a collection of advice from all the grandparents in our large family, a total of twelve. Teri and I had gathered their thoughts, planning to create a book of family wisdom for our children and all their cousins.

In reading the notes, some typed and some handwritten, I was reminded of a passage from St. John Paul II's *Letter to Families*, written in 1994. He wrote: "The history of mankind, the history of salvation passes by way of the family" (23). We as parents and grandparents prepare the next generation by teaching them to be human. Our children and grandchildren will be tomorrow's society, tomorrow's leaders, and tomorrow's Church. We prepare them through what we say and do today.

We want to share some of these gems with you.

- Regarding what is most important in life, the grandparents wrote: "Help others, especially those who need it the most." "The most important asset in life is to be an honest person at all times." "Be a good listener." "A smile goes a long way." "Spend your time and energy on what can be, not on what might have been." "Call your mother; she worries."

- On the subject of being responsible, they wrote: "If you are going to do a job, do the best job." "Take pride in what you do." "Take advantage of all the opportunities that come your way." "Doing the right thing may not always be easy but it is always right."

- About being successful, they wrote: "Success is an attitude—get yours right." "You are successful if you act like a gentleman or a lady and follow your conscience, whether you are a laborer, or a sales person, or a business executive."

- On the subject of prayer: "Faith in God is the only thing that helps us face whatever we encounter in life." "Never doubt God's willingness to forgive." "Pray—talk to God. He is a good listener." "When I doubt my faith, I ask the Blessed Mother's help in prayer." "The prayers that I find most helpful are the Our Father and the Rosary, which I recite daily."

"In God's plan the family is the first school of how to be human."
■ ST. JOHN PAUL II[17]

Our Love Story Is a Link in a Chain of Love

Pope Francis tells us that each one of us, each couple is a link in God's love story—we are a link in God's chain of love. He said: "So this love story began [in the heart of the Father], a story that has gone on for so long, and is not yet ended. We, the women and men…are in the middle of a love story; each one of us is a link in this chain of love."[18] Our love story, our marriage, is a link in a long chain of love that started at creation, unfolded in the Old Testament, reached it fullness in the person of Jesus, and continues to unfold today. Among the married couples we meet along the way in God's love story are: Adam and Eve, Abraham and Sarah, Isaac and Rebecca, Jacob and Rachel, Tobiah and Sarah, Joachim and Ann, Mary and Joseph, Sts. Louis and Zélie Martin, Blesseds Luigi and Maria Beltrame, and many others. God placed each of them at a particular point in time and at a particular place according to his plan. God also placed you and your spouse at a particular location and time for a specific purpose. Do you ever think about what God expects of you?

We are the present, a link between the past and the future, and with God's help our role is to teach our children and grandchildren how to love and to pass on to them our faith.

Your marriage is not about you. It is a relationship with a purpose that is greater than you. Pope Francis explains that a couple's life is a mission to manifest God's love to each other and to the people in their life.

"God wants to speak to the world by your life."
■ POPE FRANCIS[19]

Christ, the Bridegroom, Is Our Model

Like the couple at Cana, every marriage has six jars that need to
be filled with the good wine. In our relationship we enjoy the
taste of the good wine when we embrace six loving attitudes:
welcoming, being faithful, being generous, forgiving, showing
compassion, and serving. These are what we call the six jars of
love, and they are the essence of love according to psychologists.
No relationship can survive without even one of them. These
attitudes are so central to any love relationship that we find
them in God's love for us as revealed in the Bible. In addition we
find them in Christ's love for his Bride, the Church, as expressed
in the seven sacraments: baptism, confirmation, Eucharist, penance and reconciliation, anointing of the sick, holy orders, and
matrimony.

In the sacraments we encounter Jesus, who bathes us and
cleanses us, embraces us as members of his family, stands by us
to give us strength, feeds us, heals our sinfulness, and leads us to
the Father. The sacramental system of the Catholic Church, when
viewed from the perspective of a spousal relationship between
Christ and the Church, is a model for our loving each other as
husbands and wives. The sacraments reveal Christ's loving attitudes of welcome, faithfulness, generosity, forgiveness, compassion, and service toward his Bride, the Church, and are the point
of reference for our spousal love.[20]

- The husband or wife who warmly welcomes their spouse
  home after a long day at work or after being away expresses

the same loving attitude as Christ does when he welcomes us into his Father's family through the sacrament of baptism.

- The husband or wife who stands by their spouse to listen and to give support and honest advice in making a difficult career decision shows the same loving attitude of loyalty as Christ does for us in the sacrament of confirmation when he binds us to himself and gives us the Holy Spirit to be with us, guide us, and strengthen us.

- The husband or wife who gives up a favorite hobby to spend more time with their spouse and family gives them a taste of the same self-giving love that we experience in Christ's sacrifice in the Eucharist.

- The husband or wife who forgives their spouse for forgetting a birthday or a special event, or a promise not kept, shows the same mercy that Christ shows in the sacrament of reconciliation.

- The husband or wife who out of compassion stays up all night to care for a sick spouse or children gives them a taste of Christ's compassionate love expressed in the sacrament of the anointing of the sick.

- The couple who welcomes children, naturally or through adoption, and prepares them for life expresses the same attitude of service of God that Christ does for the Church in the sacraments of holy orders and matrimony.

What we must add is that through our participation in the sacraments, especially the Eucharist and reconciliation, we receive the graces we need to grow in these loving attitudes of welcome, faithfulness, generosity, forgiveness, compassion, and service.

In the coming chapters we will reflect on each of these loving attitudes and pray that through Christ's graces we embrace them and let them shape our behaviors and habits. Then we will enjoy the "second wine," which as John the Evangelist tells us in the Cana story, is far better than the first. The second wine helps us experience, although imperfectly, the goodness of God's love through the love of our spouse.

PRAYER

God, our Father, creator of the universe,
source of all life, and fount of love,
you placed us here on Earth and brought us together
     to serve you.
For this we thank you.

In marriage we have accepted a special role
     in your infinite design.
Although we do not understand your plan,
we ask you to open our hearts
that we may allow your Son to guide us
and your Spirit to write our story.

Help us grow in humility and obedience to you.
We ask this through Jesus, your Son.
Amen.

Together recite the Hail Mary, the Memorare, and the Glory Be (these prayers can be found on pages 10–11).

PERSONAL/COUPLE REFLECTION

Before you begin reading the next chapter, pause to reflect on how you relate to your spouse today regarding the attitudes found in the six jars of love.

1. To what degree am I welcoming, patient, understanding, and tolerant toward my spouse? (*Love welcomes*)

2. To what degree am I present and attentive to my spouse's needs? To what degree am I honest and faithful to the promises I make, even the small ones? (*Love is faithful*)

3. To what degree am I generous toward my spouse? How am I willing to make sacrifices in order to accommodate my spouse's wishes? (*Love is generous*)

4. To what degree do I forgive my spouse's actions and words that hurt or disappoint me? When I do something that hurts my spouse do I acknowledge the hurt I caused and ask forgiveness? (*Love forgives*)

5. To what degree do I seek to understand my spouse and give him/her comfort and support when in distress? (*Love is compassionate*)

6. To what degree do I eagerly help my spouse with tasks and activities in which he/she is involved? Do I understand married life as a life of service to God—a vocation? (*Love serves*)

GROUP SHARING

1. How did your love story begin? How did you meet? What were your first impressions of each other?

2. What have been key providential moments along the way in your love story?

3. What have been the moments in which you felt God's presence in your life?

4. If you were to name your love story, what title would you give it?

5. What do you think we can learn from the seven sacraments about loving our spouse?

PRACTICE

During the coming week pause from time to time to remember that God is present in your life and remind yourself to let him write your story.

Chapter 3

THE FIRST JAR OF LOVE

Love Welcomes

"I take you to be my spouse."

Married love is welcoming.
Spouses open the door of their hearts
to accept each other without any conditions,
and to welcome children with joy.

* * *

Just as in baptism Christ opens the doors of God's Kingdom
and welcomes us into his Father's family to share his life with us,
husband and wife welcome each other daily
to share a life in common.

* * *

When husband and wife accept each other's differences
and unique personalities
they become an icon of God's love in the world.

ONE OF THE GOOD HABITS I (JOHN) LEARNED AS A CHILD FROM MY MOTHER, AND FOR WHICH I AM GRATEFUL, IS CAPTURED IN AN IMAGE THAT IS FROZEN IN MY MEMORY. It is my mother's silhouette standing by an open window, looking out in the distance. Each day at 6 PM, the factory where my father worked blew a whistle to signal the end of the workday. Upon hearing the sound, my mother would call us home, set the table, and then wait at the window to spot my father in the distance coming home on his bike. When my father would walk in the house, she would tell us, "Go greet your father." As a child I did not realize the significance of this small gesture.

Welcoming each other is something we did during our wedding ceremony—"I…take you…to be my wife/husband"—and we need to continue to do it daily throughout our marriage. Unfortunately, after we are married, we forget. For example, consider what happens in your home when you or a member of your family walks in the house after having been away for a few hours. If your family is like most, the first to greet you is your dog. Does anyone else say anything? Greeting each other and welcoming each other home after a day's work, a long day of running errands, or any other excursion is beneficial to your marriage.

In our daily interactions we are constantly entering or exiting each other's lives. We do so whenever we ask a question, give a word of advice, when we reach out to give a kiss or an embrace, and through many other small interactions. It is like we are knocking at each other's door, saying, "Hey, I am here. Give me some of your time and attention," and we hope to be acknowledged. How we are received impacts our relationship.

Welcoming each other is a quality of love a marriage needs to survive. The attitude of welcome is the content of the first jar of love. We learn this welcoming attitude from God, from how Christ welcomes us into his Father's family at baptism.

The Sacrament of Baptism

At your baptism the priest or deacon said to you: "The Christian community welcomes you with great joy."[21] Then, at the close of the rite, he said: "God the Father of our Lord Jesus Christ has freed you from sin, given you a new birth by water and the Holy Spirit, and welcomed you into his holy people."[22]

Baptism is Christ's loving act of forgiveness, which, through the Holy Spirit, washes away our sins and makes us acceptable to the Father, who welcomes us into his family. It is through our baptism that we start a personal relationship with the Trinity: Father, Son, and Holy Spirit.

All relationships begin with an act of welcome that says to the other: "You are OK. I want to be with you; come into my life. I want to spend time with you and get to know you."

I Take You to Be My Spouse

Wedding ceremonies and rituals are steeped in traditions, many of which go back to the times of the Greeks and the Romans. When John and I were married, we left for our honeymoon right after the wedding ceremony and the reception. When we returned, we came back to what was to be our home, for the first time as husband and wife. As we approached the entrance to the apartment where we would live, I asked: "Are you going to carry me over the threshold? You know, it is the custom." John said. "Certainly! You are my wife, so I will."

I (John) looked up the history of this ritual, which is still popular today, and it seems to have different meanings depending on the source. For us that short conversation and gesture was almost like a renewal of our vows. With the gesture of lifting Teri up and carrying her over the threshold of my old apartment, I was welcoming her into my life and turning my small dwelling into "our new home."

The attitude of welcome and acceptance stands as the foundation of all marriage relationships. Without this attitude no marriage can grow and thrive.

Bartimaeus

Jesus is our model of this attitude of welcome and acceptance. Pope Francis explains in *The Joy of Love* (322) that when people approached Jesus he would meet their gaze directly and lovingly. Such is what happened one day while leaving the city of Jericho. Jesus came upon a blind man, Bartimaeus, who was on the side of the road begging. As he heard that Jesus was arriving, he started shouting: "Jesus, son of David, have pity on me." Jesus heard him and stopped. He reached out to Bartimaeus with a welcoming response that opened the door to a relationship: "What do you want me to do for you?" Bartimaeus said: "Master, I want to see." Jesus told him: "Go your way; your faith has saved you." With those words a relationship was started. In Mark, chapter ten we learn that Bartimaeus not only gained his sight but also followed Jesus.

How Are You Welcoming Your Spouse?

A key building block to our relationship is the way we respond to our spouse's biddings for our attention, such as when our spouse says: "What do you think?" "Did you see this?" "Give me a hand, please!" "Are you OK?" "I'm home!" Each of these biddings is like a knocking at the door of our heart. We may perceive these gestures as an opportunity to connect or as an annoying interruption. What defines our response is our attitude toward our spouse in that moment. What we say or do in those moments impacts our marriage.

If we repeatedly ignore our spouse's requests for attention, or appear to tolerate them, or if we dismiss them, our spouse will feel rejected and offended. He/she may perceive a message from us that says: "I don't care, or I don't have time for you. Don't bother me. Go away!" At that very moment our spouse may not complain, but that interaction leaves a check mark in the negative column of our relationship's balance sheet. Jesus' attitude of welcome toward Bartimaeus can be of great inspiration to us in our daily interactions: "What do you want me to do for you?"

To help you assess your habits about welcoming and accepting each other we have identified some situations that you are likely to encounter in your day. Put yourself in these situations and ask yourself, "What am I likely to do or say in these moments?" and "Is my spouse likely to feel accepted or rejected by what I do?" For example:

- Your spouse says to you:
  What do you think about what I am wearing?
  » How are you likely to respond?
  » How is your spouse likely to feel?
  A helpful door opener may be: "Let me see" or "Show me!"
  A door slammer to avoid: No response or "It doesn't matter."

- Your spouse says:
  I saw Mary, our friend, today. (Your spouse wants to start a conversation.)

> » What are you likely to say or do?
> » How is your spouse likely to feel?

A helpful door opener may be: "What did Mary say?"
or "How is she?"

A door slammer to avoid: No response or "The crazy one?"

- Your spouse says to you:
  Guess what happened at work today?
  > » What are you likely to say or do?
  > » How is your spouse likely to feel?

  A helpful door opener may be: "Tell me what happened,
  I'm curious…"

  A door slammer to avoid: "I don't know" and walk away.

- Your spouse says to you: *We don't have enough clean dishes!*
  > » What are you likely to say or do?
  > » How is your spouse likely to feel?

  A helpful door opener may be: "Would you like me
  to wash some dishes?"

  A door slammer to avoid: "Is that my fault? It was your turn
  to do the dishes!"

- Your spouse says to you: *Would you like to go for a walk?*
  > » What are you likely to say or do?
  > » How is your spouse likely to feel?

  A helpful door opener may be: "Yes, I would" or "I would,
  but can't right now; thanks for the invitation."

  A door slammer to avoid: "Not with you. You walk too
  slow!" or "No" (without an explanation).

- Your spouse says to you: *I had a terrible day today.*
    - » What are you likely to say or do?
    - » How is your spouse likely to feel?

    A helpful door opener may be: "I am sorry that you had a bad day. Tell me what happened."

    A door slammer to avoid: "Not again! Tomorrow will be better. Don't think about it now" or "I told you to quit that job!"

- Your spouse says: *I'm home!* (as your spouse walks in the house)
    - » What are you likely to say or do?
    - » How is your spouse likely to feel?

    A helpful door opener may be: "Welcome home. How are you?"

    A door slammer to avoid: No acknowledgment.

How you respond to your spouse's bidding for your attention reinforces the way you interact and forms habits that give shape to your relationship. Not all of these habits are positive.

Pay attention to these interactions. If your love for each other has become cold or distant, turning your door slammers into door openers will bring warmth and closeness. Reading this book may be an opportunity to identify some of your habits that detract from the relationship and gradually change them.

Keep in mind that welcoming each other also means accepting and accommodating one another's foibles and quirks.

The Importance of Welcoming Our Spouse's Advice

One morning, as we were nearing our thirty-eighth anniversary, Teri complimented me: "I noticed that today you hung your bath towel the right way." I was surprised and amused. Over the years I have learned of many ways I can improve myself, but I never thought that my way of folding the bath towel was one. I did not know there was a wrong way to hang a bath towel. Teri proceeded to explain the reason why she wanted the towel folded in a particular way, and it made sense to me. This was all said in fun, and we both laughed. Since then I have been folding the bath towel the way she showed me. I am sharing this incident not to criticize Teri but to emphasize that spouses learn from each other.

Being able to accept gracefully the influence of one's spouse is part of the secret of marital success. This observation comes from Dr. John Gottman, a researcher who spent over forty years studying couples. He directs his advice specifically to husbands. In his studies with couples he found that men who are willing to accept the influence of their wives are happily married. Those who are not willing to accept her influence see their marriages become unstable.[23] He writes: "[In our research] we did find that the happiest, most stable marriages in the long run were those where the husband treated his wife with respect and did not resist power sharing and decision making with her."[24]

In other words, men: listen to your wives. They are your partners. You live in the same home; open the door and let them into your life so that they can contribute to helping you become a better man. Yes, each of us has the mission from God to help our spouse become a better person.

"The husband has the duty of making the wife more of a woman and the wife has the duty of making the husband more of a man....This is called growing together." ■ **POPE FRANCIS**[25]

Sometimes to Be Welcomed We Need to Knock Gently

While listening to your spouse's advice is a good idea, it is sometimes difficult to receive the advice because of the way it is delivered. When the advice is delivered in a way that hurts, it is important to take a deep breath and avoid striking back to get even. If you are taken aback by the tone of the advice, acknowledge to your spouse that you heard the message, and share how you feel without accusing. (i.e., "I am surprised by the tone of your voice. I did not realize you were so upset."), and then proceed to discuss the subject, addressing your spouse with respect. However, if you are too emotional in that moment to talk about the subject rationally, agree with your spouse to discuss it at a different time. Give yourself time to calm down. The rule to remember is mutual respect.

On the other hand, if we want to be heard, we may need to knock gently, especially if the advice is a suggestion or a correction. When we need to speak to our spouse and want to be sure that he or she welcomes us and listens to us, we need to choose our timing and our words carefully. Dr. Gottman writes that in his research he found that eighty percent of the time the wife is the one who brings up sticky marital issues, while the husband tries to avoid them. He comments that this is not a symptom of a troubled marriage—it is true in most happy marriages as well.

Some time ago, we interviewed several couples and asked them, "How do you approach your spouse when you want to bring up a difficult subject?" What each couple answered was very practical and insightful.

One wife said: "I wait for the right time. I don't approach my spouse as he walks in the door coming home from work. I give him a chance to relax and I look for a time when he's ready for a serious conversation. Choosing the right time is very important."

A husband said: "I make an effort to choose the right words so that I can be heard. I may even practice what I want to say."

A wife said: "I prepare by praying to the Holy Spirit to give me the right words and for my husband to have the right attitude and hear what I want to say."

Another wife said: "I prepare a nice meal, and then after the meal I say: I need to talk to you about something important to me."

To be heard, especially when we have something to say that may be difficult for our spouse to hear, we need to find the right time and to approach our spouse with an attitude of respect. If we feel angry and want to shout, social scientists such as Dr. Gottman recommend taking time to cool off before trying to address a conflict.[26]

"Making a point should never involve venting anger and inflicting hurt." ■ **POPE FRANCIS**[27]

Mutual Acceptance Is Based on Respect

The essence of welcoming and accepting each other is respect; respect for oneself and respect for the unique person that your spouse is. Accepting your spouse does not mean agreeing with your spouse or tolerating all his or her annoying habits. You are different individuals with different family histories, distinct personalities, upbringings, and education. You will disagree often. Acceptance often means living with some of the discomfort brought about by our different opinions, feelings, habits, traits, and preferences. That is respect. Respect is what allows you to disagree without injuring your relationship.

The differences that exist between you and your spouse are what make you unique as a couple. They give a special flavor to your lifestyle. Do not suppress those differences but manage them. Your differences will cause many conflicts. Acknowledge your conflicts openly; solve those that you can, and learn to live with the others.

Dr. Gottman writes in *The Seven Principles for Making Marriage Work* that all marital conflicts fall into two categories: those that can be resolved, and those that keep on recurring. Unfortunately, adds Dr. Gottman, sixty-nine percent of all conflicts fall into the category of recurring. He lists five typical recurring conflicts he found in happy couples:

1. One spouse wants to have a baby; the other is not ready.

2. One wants to have sex more frequently than the other.

3. One is not keen on doing chores; the other nags.

4. One wants to raise the children in one religious tradition; the other wants to raise them in a different one.

5. One is more strict in disciplining the children; the other is more lax.[28]

What are the recurring conflicts in your marriage?

PRAYER

Loving Jesus, your first miracle was at Cana
for a married couple who did not know they had a problem.

We come to you, holding our jar of welcome,
aware of how much we need your help.

We humbly ask you to bless us and help us fill our marriage
with daily gestures of welcome toward each other,
tender smiles, greeting each other at the door,
loving words, and warm embraces.

Help us to remember to always keep the door
*   of our hearts open to each other*
even in the midst of our daily busyness,
knowing that the love we share is a gift from you.

Amen.

Together recite the Hail Mary, the Memorare, and the Glory Be (these prayers can be found on pages 10–11).

PERSONAL/COUPLE REFLECTION

In this chapter we reflected on the content of the first jar of love: the attitude of welcome. We pondered specifically on behaviors that are the building blocks of our relationship: how we acknowledge each other, how we bid for each other's attention, and how we respond to each other's requests. Spend some time reflecting on the following situations, remembering Jesus' words to Bartimaeus: "What do you want me to do for you?" (Mark 10:51).

Consider what happens in the following recurring interactions with your spouse. Do so individually and then together as a couple.

Interaction 1: Greeting

- *How do I greet my spouse when he/she leaves the house or returns home?*
- *How would I like to be greeted?*

Interaction 2: Responding to interruptions

- *How do I feel when my spouse interrupts me while I am talking or when I am doing something?*
- *How would I like my spouse to act when he/she needs to interrupt me?*

Interaction 3: Listening to our spouse's suggestions

- *How do I feel when my spouse makes a suggestion or gives me advice?*
- *How would I like my spouse to approach me with a suggestion or words of advice?*

Interaction 4: Asking for a favor

- *How does my spouse respond when I ask a question or a favor?*
- *Find out from your spouse how he/she wants to be approached when you need something.*

GROUP SHARING

1. In what ways are the actions of Christ in baptism parallel to the actions of spouses in marriage?

2. What are typical conflicts you encounter because you and your spouse have different preferences or ways of doing things?

3. How do you resolve your differences? Share with the members of your group what works for you and what does not work well for you.

4. Are you able to stop yourself and take a break when your emotions get heated?

5. How might the story of Bartimaeus and Jesus' words to him be a good model for you to remember? What did Jesus say to Bartimaeus?

PRACTICE

This week develop the habit of welcoming each other with a kiss upon waking and before going to bed, and during the day, compliment each other with affirming words.

Chapter 4

THE SECOND JAR OF LOVE
Love Is Faithful

*"I promise to be faithful to you
in good times and in bad."*

*Married love binds.
Spouses belong to one another.
They promise to be present and loyal to each other
and to always keep their word.*

* * *

*Just as in confirmation Christ
binds us to himself and is present
to us through the gift of the Holy Spirit,
in marriage husband and wife bind themselves to one another
with the promise to be always true and present to each other.*

* * *

*When husband and wife are true to each other
they become an icon of Christ's faithful love for his Bride,
the Church.*

WE ASKED COUPLES: HOW DO YOU STAY FAITHFUL TO EACH OTHER?
How do you keep your relationship with friends and coworkers
of the opposite sex from interfering with your marriage?

Lorie, the wife of a photojournalist for a prominent news
network, spoke first. "Mike works with the most glamorous and
beautiful women in the city. Some days he goes on a day-trip
with a reporter to cover a story. I trust him, but at times I wonder:
'what are they talking about during those long car rides together?
Where do they eat lunch together?'"

Mike agrees: "This can be an issue. When I go to work, I may
be assigned to work with a young, pretty reporter. We will be
gone for the day to cover a story and work closely for eight to ten
hours, just the two of us. These working conditions create a little
bit of tension between Lorie and me. For example, if the reporter
and I decided to eat at a restaurant like the Olive Garden, Lorie
would consider the setting too intimate."

He adds, "I would never do anything that would betray Lorie
and our marriage. When there is a gray area, a situation that I
think could make Lorie uncomfortable, I tell her up front. We
have no secrets. We share the password to our cell phones and
Internet accounts. We want to be honest with each other and not
hide anything. That is the only way to protect our relationship."

Married love is faithful, loyal, honest, and requires constant
presence to each other. Faithfulness is the attitude contained in
the second jar of love.

The Marriage Commitment Demands Honesty

Love brings two lovers together. Marriage binds them, makes
them one. They belong to each other. Their bond is a commitment to faithfulness and honesty.

Honesty is the foundation of all relationships, especially the marital relationship. Yet, in our daily interactions, we easily find ourselves engaging in behaviors that are not honest. For example, have you ever found yourself fudging the truth or embellishing facts when answering a question from your spouse that made you uncomfortable? Or, in a moment when your spouse was pressing you to do something, have you ever said: "Yes, I'll take care of it," but you had no intention of doing it? Or, have you hidden purchases from your spouse to avoid a conflict?

These, although small, are deceitful acts. They are negative interactions that cause the relationship to deteriorate, especially if they take residence in your life as habits. Whenever we are not truthful, or we do not intend to do what we say, we fail what we promised in our vow: "I promise to be faithful to you in good times and in bad."

We learn faithfulness from Christ in the sacrament of confirmation.

The Sacrament of Confirmation

Do you remember the day of your confirmation? At your confirmation the bishop called on the Father to send the Holy Spirit to dwell in you and to help you conform your life to Christ's. Then he marked you with oil as a sign that you belong to Christ. He traced a cross on your forehead with blessed oil, marking you like a shepherd marks his sheep. He said: "Be sealed with the Gift of the Holy Spirit." You belong to Christ, he is your shepherd, and you are a member of his flock, enrolled in his service, and enjoying his protection (CCC, 1296).

In the sacrament of confirmation Christ binds us to himself and promises his constant presence to us through the Holy Spirit. That is faithfulness.

I Promise to Be Faithful to You

There is no greater proof of the power of the marriage bond than being with a couple that is celebrating their fiftieth wedding anniversary.

Some time ago we were invited to attend Jim and Norma's fiftieth wedding anniversary celebration. Months before, fighting the odds of advanced cancer, Jim promised Norma: "I will be here for our anniversary. Let's plan a big celebration with our friends and family." So, they did. That evening Jim and Norma were surrounded by their children, grandchildren, and friends to renew their vows and to celebrate their life together, knowing that Jim's end was near. Dressed in a tuxedo, Jim was beaming, although physically weak. He mustered all of his strength to get up and dance with Norma, his daughters, and his eight-year-old granddaughter. After each dance he would return to his seat for some oxygen.

Jim and Norma's life is a tribute to love and to Christian marriage. We got to know them when we led a marriage preparation weekend with them. We still remember them sharing with the engaged couples their struggles to understand and adjust to each other's unique personalities. They both had to pause to dry their tears as they narrated their battles and the tender moments of their life. Their commitment prevailed, and their life together was a witness to all of us of what faithful married love is about. Their loyalty and honesty were admirable.

Your Wedding Ring

Just as in confirmation the bishop marked you with oil as a sign that you belong to Christ, during your wedding ceremony you and your spouse marked each other with a ring, a symbol of your belonging to one another with a promise of fidelity for the rest of your life.

The commitment we made on our wedding day is a covenant. When we exchanged our rings we said: "Receive this ring as a sign of my love and fidelity. In the name of the Father, and of the Son, and of the Holy Spirit." In our Catholic ceremony our exchange of rings is not just a ritual between two people; it is one that involves God. Through our vow we made a covenant with each other and with God. In that moment we entered the mystery of God's love and were embraced by him. The Holy Spirit bound us together, and our marriage became part of Christ's unbreakable marriage covenant with his Bride, the Church. This is why your marriage covenant is unbreakable.[29]

The Good Shepherd

In the Gospel of John, Jesus gives us an image of faithfulness and trustworthiness. It is the good shepherd (John 10:1–18). This image at first glance does not seem to relate to marriage. In reality it does because it is about faithfulness, honesty, dependability, and self-sacrifice. The good shepherd is totally committed to his sheep. He has nothing to hide. He is not devious. He enters the sheepfold through the main gate, says Jesus, unlike a thief who climbs sneakily over the fence. There is an intimate bond between the good shepherd and the sheep. Jesus tells us that the sheep recognize his voice and follow him; they trust him because they can count on him to lead them on the right path to safe pastures.

The image of the good shepherd applies to marriage because spouses are shepherds to each other and to their children. In our respective roles as husband and wife, we are called to guide and protect each other, like the shepherd does his sheep. However, to be successful we need to be present and hide nothing from each other. We need to keep our word because our spouse and children want to be able to count on us and to trust what we say.

The promise you made at your wedding is the promise of the good shepherd to his sheep: I promise to be faithful to you in good times and in bad. The love of the shepherd for his sheep is the love of Jesus for us, his Church. It is a love that binds.

"The Lord is my shepherd
There is nothing I lack.
He guides me along right paths."
■ **PSALM 23:1, 3**

Fall and Redemption

Bernie and Christine are a young couple, married just over ten years, and parents to four children. Bernie started our conversation with a confession: "Three and a half years ago I was involved in an extramarital affair." I (John) was not aware of this when I walked into their home to interview them for a video Teri and I were working on, and I was taken aback by the honesty and the regret expressed by this young man. He continued while sitting next to his wife: "During that time I was convinced that I had found the person I wanted to be with for the rest of my life, and it was not my wife!" His wife, Christine, was holding back her tears, remembering the painful experience. She explained: "I found out about it six months after the affair started." Bernie continued: "During that time I felt a deep emptiness, like I had never experienced before. I could see the pain I was causing my wife and my children, but I persisted with my relationship."

"Looking back," said Bernie, "it was a very dark time in my life. I was frozen, lying in that bed, day after day, feeling paralyzed. I felt like I was in a catch-22 where I felt I could not go in any direction and be OK."

Christine added: "So, I had to stay trusting in God through all those months...months of him not checking in. He had checked out!"

I asked both of them what had been the turning point. Bernie said: "As time progressed, I invited God back into my life. I realized that he sends his Holy Spirit to fortify our marriage and to give us courage. I am so happy for Christine sticking by me because during that time that I would not wish upon anyone, I faced a real struggle of discernment to let God truly enter my life. I had so many blessings as a result of that experience. I never imagined that an affair would happen in our marriage, but it did, and we are standing here today as strong as we have ever been as a result of that. It is all because of God."

I asked: "How is your relationship today?" Christine answered first: "It took a long time to rebuild that trust, and sometimes I still wonder and have trust issues, and I have to offer them up, and I know that he probably has his issues from time to time too. We all do. And that is when we have to wake up in the morning and commit before our feet hit the floor."

Bernie continued: "Deep down in our hearts we know what we need to do. We need to be honest with each other and find quality time together and keep God in our life."

The Power of the Promise

When I (John) was writing the book *Blessed Is Marriage*, I asked Archbishop Kurtz of Louisville to write a few words of endorsement. What the archbishop penned became the foreword to the book. In his comments he quoted a passage from Thornton Wilder, the playwright, and he added a few words of his own. We had been using Thornton Wilder's passage in our retreats, and really liked what Archbishop Kurtz added. Here is the passage:

I didn't marry you because you were perfect…
I married you because you gave me a promise.

That promise made up for your faults.
And the promise I gave you made up for mine.

Two imperfect people got married,
and it was the promise that made the marriage.
And when our children were growing up,
it wasn't a house that protected them;…
it was that promise.[30]

Archbishop Kurtz added:

And I believe that the power to live that promise
is a grace beyond us…
It is the power of God…
Guiding us through the joys and sorrows of our marriage.

The Importance of Transparency

One day while Teri and I were mentoring a group of young couples preparing for marriage, the conversation turned toward family finances. Two words that resonated among all of the engaged couples were: "transparency" and "honesty" in managing their money. They told us that honesty and transparency is what they aspired to have in their marriages.

Their comments brought to mind an image from my youth. It was the image of the kitchen table in my boyhood home in Italy. My parents and my grandparents (my mom's parents) lived together in adjoining apartments and shared some of their expenses. My family mistrusted banks because, during the Second World War, which had just ended, many banks had failed. So all their money was kept in the home—and not under the proverbial mattress but under the kitchen table. To keep their cash in a safe place, my father built a special box, which he attached under the tabletop of the kitchen table. Access to the cash was possible only by removing the heavy slab of granite that was our tabletop. The granite slab was so heavy that no one person alone could remove it from the table. It required at least two persons. This ensured the safety of the money and transparency among family members and mutual accountability.

Transparency and honesty are important in all aspects of married life, including finances. Unfortunately, too many spouses fall short in this area, according to researchers. Diane L. Danois, JD, an expert in Family Law, writes in an article on "Financial Infidelity" that a survey of 24,000 men and women found that almost 50% of married adults, 37% of men and 56% of women, admitted keeping money secrets from their spouses.

Financial planner Douglas J. Eaton offers the following tips for couples.

1. Be completely honest about any money owed.

2. Set a regular time (weekly, monthly, quarterly) to discuss the family finances.

3. Both partners should be involved in paying household bills, as this creates checks and balances.

4. Limit or eliminate individual accounts (bank, credit, etc.) and make them joint, and agree that both spouses have access to online accounts.

The National Endowment for Financial Education and the National Foundation for Credit Counseling encourage couples to make all the financial decisions together as a team. They also suggest that couples agree on a dollar amount that each spouse can spend "no questions asked" (as long as it fits in the budget).

Honesty is essential in marriage. It is the foundation of the mutual trust that holds the bond of marriage together.

Sometimes speaking the truth means saying things that your spouse does not like to hear. This is very difficult and requires a lot of diplomacy and tact. When this happens ask Mary and Jesus to help you choose the right time, the right place, and the right words—words that build up trust rather than tear it down.

Keep Your Promises, Big and Small

Keeping our promises is just as important as speaking the truth. Keeping our word helps our spouse realize that he/she can count on us and trust us. It is through our truthfulness and dependability that we develop our voice—the voice of the good shepherd. St. John the Evangelist writes that the sheep "follow him because they recognize his voice" (John 10:4). Our spouse, our children, and our friends will follow our voice, our thoughts, suggestions, and example, if they know that we tell the truth and can be trusted to do what we say we would do. Keeping our word is an important part of our faithfulness.

Bill, a friend of ours, told us about an unfortunate moment early in his marriage. He said: "Regrettably, in forty-one years of marriage there have been times when I made promises that I didn't keep. One that I can remember happened shortly after we had our first baby. One day I saw a car, an old '56 Chevy, and I just wanted it. Oh, how I wanted it! Sandy didn't want the car, and we really couldn't afford it. So, I said to Sandy: OK, I'll pass. I won't buy it. We went home. But later that day I went back by myself, I bought the car, and I drove it home. That wasn't good for our marriage...."

When we fail to keep our word we erode the trust that our spouse has in us. We create a hole in our relationship that drains the energies of the marriage, as our friend Bill learned. He said: "The classy '56 Chevy was left in the garage most of the time because whenever I spoke of using it, Sandy's hurt feelings about my broken promise would be stirred up, and tension would rise in the relationship." Bill ended up selling his prized car without making any money on it.

Friendly Advice

We close this chapter with some friendly advice from mature couples who are members of our parish. We asked them: "What do you do to protect the bond of your marriage when at work or with friends of the opposite sex?"

- "In relationships with friends and colleagues of the opposite sex I set boundaries. I am kind but clear."

- "I make sure that I don't send the wrong message, that nothing I say or do can be misconstrued as purposeful flirting."

- "I never say anything negative about my spouse or my marriage."

- A businessman who travels a lot said: "I try to avoid situations that can lead to temptations. I try to stay out of bars. You never know if you have been drinking too much." Then he added: "Now and again, I say a prayer: Lord, help me through this situation."

- "When on the Internet I am careful not to let my curiosity get the best of me. I don't post on Facebook all the details of my life."

- "Sometimes I am attracted to pornography on the Internet. So I have installed filters."

- "When traveling I keep my ring prominent. I want people to know that I belong with my husband."

Depend on the Holy Spirit to Help You Be Faithful

Being truthful and keeping our word are dimensions of faithfulness, the loving attitude that binds spouses together. Honesty touches many aspects of our marital relationship and helps us strengthen our bond. Yet each day we meet temptations to lie, to hide the facts, to exaggerate or distort the truth, to make excuses, to blame others, or to ignore what we promised because it is inconvenient. To be faithful we need the courage to always be honest and responsible. Pope Francis said: "The path of Christian courage is a grace given by the Holy Spirit" (April 13, 2015). At confirmation, we received the Holy Spirit and his gift of fortitude, also known as courage, one of the Seven Gifts. Today, the Holy Spirit stands with us ready to give us the courage we need. It is important to turn to him for help, especially when we find it difficult to be honest or to keep a promise.

In this chapter we reflected on the content of the second jar of love: faithfulness, the attitude that demands honesty and dependability. Jesus taught his disciples: "Let your 'Yes' mean 'Yes,' and 'No' mean 'No.' Anything more is from the evil one" (Matthew 5:37).

PRAYER

Jesus, our way and truth and life,
your love for us led you to the cross at Calvary.
You are our model of love that is most faithful and true.

We offer to you our jar of faithfulness
and ask you to bless us and fill our marriage
with truth and fidelity to you and to each other.

Send your Spirit to strengthen us
when we are faced with temptations, large and small,
that can hurt or damage our relationship.

Help us to always keep each other
first in our hearts and in our minds,
aware that the love we share is a gift from you.

Amen.

Together recite the Hail Mary, the Memorare, and the Glory Be (these prayers can be found on pages 10–11).

PERSONAL/COUPLE REFLECTION

Take time to reflect on the following situations that are likely to happen in your daily life, and consider the wisest way to act.

1. What do you do when you see something you want to buy for yourself but you know that your spouse would object?
   a. You buy it and hide it from your spouse.
   b. You do not buy it and resent it.
   c. You do not buy it and let your spouse know that you wish you could have it.
   d. Other…

   Ask your spouse what they would prefer for you to do when you see something you want and you think that your spouse might object to the purchase.

2. What do you do when your spouse says to you: "Where are you going?"
   a. You let the question annoy you and respond with a sarcastic remark.
   b. You explain kindly.
   c. You take offense and refuse to answer.
   d. Other…

   Discuss with your spouse whether this situation happens in your marriage. If it does, agree on the best way to address it without causing friction or creating mistrust.

3. When you say that you are going to do something, what can your spouse expect from you?
    a. You do it promptly.
    b. You will eventually get it done.
    c. You may or may not get it done.
    d. Other...

Ask your spouse how they feel about your typical way of carrying out your promises. Does your spouse have any suggestions?

4. When your spouse asks for your help, what response is he/she likely to get from you?
    a. A prompt response.
    b. A halfhearted response.
    c. An excuse for not helping.
    d. Other...

Ask your spouse if he/she is OK with your typical response. Does your spouse have any suggestions for you?

GROUP SHARING

1. How important is honesty in a marriage?

2. Is there such a thing as too much honesty? Are there things that you, as a spouse do not need to know? Explain your answer.

3. Can you think of sensitive situations in which you may want to color the truth in order not to worry or upset your spouse? What are some of these situations? Is it OK to color the truth to avoid causing some pain to your spouse?

4. As a group identify some ways in which you can, with honesty, give bad news to your spouse.

5. Is it better not to promise than to make a promise you may not be able to keep? What do you think?

6. Do you agree with the authors that there is a parallel between the sacrament of confirmation and the bond of marriage? In what ways?

7. Do you think that Jesus' image of the good shepherd applies to the lives of husbands and wives? If so, in what ways?

PRACTICE

During the coming week be intentional about being honest in what you say to your spouse, and make a strong effort to keep your promises.

Chapter 5

THE THIRD JAR OF LOVE

Love Is Generous

*"I will love you and honor you
all the days of my life."*

*Married love is generous.
Spouses make sacrifices to accommodate each other.
They rearrange their life so they can become one.*

* * *

*Just as in the Eucharist Christ
gives himself totally to us to make us holy,
in marriage husband and wife
give themselves totally to each other
to make one another better persons.*

* * *

*When husband and wife make sacrifices
for each other or for the relationship
they taste the pain of the crucifixion
and the goodness of God's self-giving love.*

69

IN EARLY SUMMER 2006, WE DECIDED TO VISIT JOHN'S FATHER, WHO LIVED IN HIS HOMETOWN IN ITALY. At age ninety-four he was well but growing weaker. When we called him to announce our trip he was very pleased and commented: "Since you will be here I want to invite the whole family to a dinner together. I will plan it and pay for it. It will be our *'ultima cena,'*" which in Italian means "last supper." We laughed at his humor.

My father made all the arrangements. When the day came, we drove outside the town to an old farmhouse turned into a restaurant. It was wonderful for the family to be together: my sister, my brother, their spouses, children and grandchildren, a total of fifteen persons. We enjoyed each other's company, shared food, and told stories. The meal lasted a whole afternoon. In the middle of it, my father left the table and went to the car to take a short nap; then he returned for dessert and coffee.

It was a meal we will always remember, especially because it truly was our last family meal with my father: our *"ultima cena."* Six weeks later we received a call that he had passed away.

Every meal we share together with our family is a celebration of life, which is made possible only because of the sacrifices of many. Our first act of generosity and sacrifice around a meal is that of giving up other commitments to make time to be together. The meal itself is also the fruit of the sacrifices made by all those who have labored to prepare it, and by the produce and the creatures of which we partake. The ritual of eating together builds our communion and sustains our life.

The generosity and self-sacrifice we experience around the family table is the love attitude that we learn from Christ in the Eucharist. It is the content of the third jar of love.

The Generosity of Christ in the Eucharist

Four words strike us when we participate in the Mass. At the Consecration we hear the words proclaimed: "*Take* this all of you....for this is my body which will be *given up for you.*" And "*Take* this all of you...this is the chalice of my blood, the blood of the new and eternal covenant, which will be *poured out for you* and for many for the forgiveness of sins."

These are the words that Jesus said at the Last Supper, the first Eucharistic celebration. They express an attitude of total self-giving. They are the words of the new covenant and resemble the words of the covenant pronounced by the bride and the groom in their Catholic wedding.

"I, N., take you, N., to be my wife/husband.
I promise to be faithful to you,
in good times and in bad,
in sickness and in health,
to love you and honor you all the days of my life."

In the books of the Old Testament the relationship of Yahweh and his people Israel, and in the New Testament the relationship of Christ and the Church, are described as a marriage relationship. The words of Jesus repeated at the Mass during the Consecration are the words of a marriage covenant between Christ, the Bridegroom, and his Bride, the Church. The Church teaches us that the marriage covenant of husband and wife, which we enter at our wedding is a participation in the divine covenant of Christ and the Church.[31] This is why Christian marriage is permanent; the promises we make cannot be dissolved.

The Church teaches us that "authentic married love is caught up into divine love."[32] These are wonderful words from a document of the Second Vatican Council.[33] However, these lofty words make us wonder: How can our marriage be caught up in the divine love when we fight and argue and sometimes hurt each other? The answer is that our sacramental marriage is truly a participation in Christ's covenant, and at the same time we are human and imperfect, needing his help to become what God made us to be. We are a work in progress. Pope Francis tells us that through the Eucharist Christ wants to enter into our life and fill it with his graces.[34]

"I promise to love you and to honor you all the days of my life"

What we learn from Jesus in the Eucharist is how to love our spouse. Pope Benedict XVI writes that self-giving love seeks the good of the beloved and is even willing to make sacrifices for the good of the spouse.[35]

A friend of ours, Bill, lay dying in the hospital, going in and out of consciousness. He was battling a serious form of cancer. During a moment of clarity he whispered to Carol, one his friends who was standing at his bedside, "Next week is my wife Roberta's birthday. I was planning to do something big for her. If I cannot be there to organize the festivities would you do that for me?" Then after a pause, he continued: "On her birthday I want you to take Bert for a manicure and a massage, and then invite all the neighbors and friends to our house for a party. I want her birthday to be a joyful occasion." Bill died two days later.

On Roberta's birthday we all gathered at the family's home, and although we were sad, we celebrated with music, hot dogs, grilled chicken, hamburgers, and cake and ice cream. Bill would have been the life of the party, but he was only present in spirit, and we all learned a lesson from him. His love for Roberta was such that he was looking out for her even as he was dying. He wanted his wife's birthday not to be shadowed by his death. Love is overlooking what I want and doing what is good for my spouse.

"Love seeks the good of the beloved."
■ **POPE BENEDICT XVI**[36]

What Does Self-Giving Love Look Like?

On a Friday afternoon, as I walked by my friend Charlie's office I asked him: "Do you have big plans for the weekend?" He smiled, nodding, and then he shook his head as if to say, "Don't ask!" I waited without saying anything. I was curious. Charlie explained: "Mary and I are going to spend the weekend with a buddy of mine who was my college roommate. He and his wife live in Memphis."

"That should be fun," I said. "Yes, I'm sure it will be," said Charlie under his breath. "There's just one problem," he continued. "I found out last night that Mary doesn't like my friend's wife. We've been planning this trip for weeks, and yesterday she told me: 'I really don't want to go on this trip...' and she proceeded to explain her dislike for the lady who'll be our host." Charlie raised his head and looked at me, saying: "I understand Mary's feelings, but it's too late to back out of this situation. My friend in Memphis already purchased tickets for concert events and made arrangements for us to stay with them at their home."

"I understand your situation," I said. "What are you going to do?"

"I'll talk to Mary this evening," he said. "We'll plan our schedule so as to make the event as pleasant as possible for her. We have been married for over twenty years and we have known this couple since college. I never knew Mary has a dislike for this person."

I left saying: "I'm sure you'll make the best of it."

As I walked away after listening to Charlie's story, I had a smile on my face. I was touched by his thoughtfulness toward Mary. As he was telling me about his predicament he never made a critical or disparaging remark about her. Although I could feel the discomfort this situation was causing him, all I heard from him were words of concern for Mary. With this trip he wanted to reconnect with his former college roommate, but he did not want this opportunity to be at his wife's expense. In fact, he said that if he had known about Mary's dislike even just the week before, he would have canceled the trip.

Generosity and Sacrifice

The third jar of love contains the attitude of self-giving and sacrifice. A report published by the National Marriage Project at the University of Virginia states that spouses who embrace a spirit of generosity and sacrifice in their marriage enjoy higher-quality marriages. The researchers define generosity as: "the virtue of giving good things to one's spouse freely and abundantly."[37] Doing so requires sacrifice. So, why do we do it?

Your Marriage Is Your Treasure

We asked couples what sacrifices they make in their daily life to accommodate their spouse. A wife surprised us with her insightful response: "The things I do for Steve do not feel like sacrifices. I do what I do because I love him. I do it willingly because in the long run it is good for me and for our relationship." She was saying that sacrifices do not feel like sacrifices when we see our marriage as something worth sacrificing for, something valuable like a treasure.

In chapter thirteen of the Gospel of Matthew we find a collection of parables told by Jesus to describe God's Kingdom. One of them is about a man who finds a treasure. "The kingdom of heaven is like a treasure buried in a field, which a person finds and hides again, and out of joy goes and sells all that he has and buys that field" (Matthew 13:44).

Your marriage is your treasure. When you were dating you discovered a relationship so precious to you that you wanted to have it for the rest of your life. To obtain it you made a radical decision. Like the man in the parable, you invested all of yourself into it, and you got married. You rearranged your life's priorities; you even gave up some of your freedom, because the relationship you had with your spouse was a worthy treasure. Such self-giving brought you joy.

In this chapter we will reflect on two aspects of married life that help us treat our marriage as our treasure: investing time in each other, and eating meals together. Both are essential to the health of the marriage relationship, and both require an attitude of generosity and self-giving, and even sacrifice.

Investing Time in Each Other

Michele Weiner-Davis writes in her book *Divorce Busting*, "The single biggest contributor to the breakdowns in relationships today is the fact that couples aren't spending enough time together. They are not making their relationship a number one priority."[38]

A practice that many marriage experts are recommending to couples is that of continuing to go on dates after the wedding. A report by the National Marriage Project titled "The Date Night Opportunity"[39] finds that the practice of dating strengthens marriages. Bradford Wilcox and Jeffrey Dew, the authors of the report, write, "Couples who devote time specifically to one another at least once a week are markedly more likely to enjoy high-quality relationships and lower divorce rates." This practice has the potential of strengthening a marriage in at least five ways:

> *Communication*—Couple time can "foster much needed communication, mutual understanding and a sense of communion between the spouses."

> *Novelty*—Date nights can break the monotony of daily life through activities that are new and fun for both.

> *Eros*—Going on a date can help spouses rekindle their romantic spark.

> *Commitment*—Time alone together solidifies the spouses' commitment to each other.

> *De-Stress*—Getting away from the concerns of daily life relieves a couple's stresses.

Having one-on-one couple time with your spouse does not have to cost a lot of money. For example, you can plan something fun together after the children go to bed. That is what Teri and I used to do when our children were young, and we still do from time to time. We like to play Double Solitaire and UNO. Over the years when we played UNO, we tracked and dated our scores on a pad that we keep with the cards. When we play now, we find ourselves leafing through the pages looking back at our individual scores and the scores of family and friends who played with us, and who won when. They bring back fond memories.

A couple told us that when their children were young the only time alone together they could carve out for themselves was once a week when they would get a babysitter to go grocery shopping.

Whatever your schedules, and whatever the stresses you experience because of all the demands placed on you, make sure to create rituals that connect the two of you together and foster a sense of communion.

Family Meals

One family ritual that nourishes the emotional and physical needs of spouses and family members is eating meals together.

Eating together is a ritual that reminds us of what we do during Mass. At church we remember our common story of salvation in the death and resurrection of Jesus, we break bread together as a sign of unity, and we eat Christ's body as nourishment for our spiritual life. The ritual of the Eucharist strengthens our relationship with the Trinity, with all the members of the assembly, and with the whole Church. We are all one family around Christ's table.

Eating together is a human activity that nourishes not only our bodies but also our relationships. If you want to strengthen your bond with your spouse and your family and increase your intimacy, use your meal times as an opportunity for sharing your stories, the events of your day, or simply for being quiet together and enjoying the safety of each other's company.

So, let us ask:

1. How often do you and your family have a meal together?

2. During your meals is your TV turned on?

3. Do you keep your cell phone, e-mails, and text messages from interrupting your meal?

4. Do you pray before your meal?

Having regular meals together is not only beneficial to your marriage but also to your children. Anne Fishel, PhD, founder of The Family Dinner Project and author of *Home for Dinner*, writes that meals together may be the only time during the day when we can reconnect, leave behind our individual pursuits, recharge, laugh, tell stories, and catch up with the ups and downs of each other's day.[40]

Unfortunately, various reports indicate that the practice of eating meals together as a family is slowly vanishing. Cody Delistaty writes in an article in *The Atlantic* that the Norman Rockwell painting of the family at the table together, once the image of life in the middle class, is now considered obsolete, an image from the past. The reasons are obvious: the lack of time, two careers, our children's activities, and so on. Social scientists encourage parents to review their priorities. Eating meals together regularly is one of the best things parents can do for their children's social development, health, and academic performance.

A study conducted by the National Center on Addiction and Substance Abuse at Columbia University found that children who eat dinner with their parents five or more times a week have less trouble with drugs and alcohol, eat healthier foods, show better academic performance, and report being closer to their parents.[41]

We encourage you to be resourceful. Be creative in how you make time for each other. We met a single-parent family that recognized the importance of eating meals together as a family; not having the flexibility of serving a regular dinner, they decided to make breakfast their family meal. Every morning before leaving for work or school, everyone gathers at the family table to share breakfast together. Other families adapt to the demands of modern life, such as business travels and working on different shifts, by making the point of having a family meal at least on Saturday or Sunday.

Watch Out for Distractions

Today, most couples and families struggle not only to find the time to have fun together or to eat a meal as a family, but also to keep the distractions of TV, cell phones, e-mail, and text messages from interfering with their relationships. Yes, it is hard to unplug, but we must if we want to stay connected with one another.

One evening while eating at a restaurant we noticed a family with three young children seated at a table near us. They each, including the parents, spent their entire meal looking at their tablet or cell phone. What a missed opportunity!

Our digital devices are useful to us, but we must learn to use them judiciously; otherwise, they become intruders that take over the time we have for each other.

Marriage therapists are seeing more and more couples who report relationship problems related to digital technology. The dangers of digital technology are many, but three stand out.[42]

Digital technology is addictive. It pulls us in. There is always something new to see. Just one more moment, one more e-mail, one more text, one more picture…and time passes.

Skewed priorities. The pull of digital technology causes us to develop skewed priorities. Activities and people who should be central to our world become second to our digital connections. For example, we may be in the habit of interrupting a face-to-face conversation to check a text message just received.

Social boundaries are blurred. When in front of a screen or a camera we seem to lose the sense of prudence and judgment in what we say and do. Dr. Dave Currie writes in a blog that this weakness becomes dangerous when we start flirting with others, engage in sexual talk, dirty jokes, sharing intimate information, exchanging questionable photos, and engaging in other behaviors that draw us inadvertently closer to another person than to our mate.

Dr. Currie suggests some practical boundaries to help couples protect their marriage.[43] Among these are:

- No electronics, including calls, texts, or TV, during mealtime;

- No electronics while a family member wants to discuss a concern or problem;

- No electronics while your spouse is driving. Be in the moment with them;

- If you are expecting an important work-related call, give notice to your spouse.

In this chapter we reflected on generosity, the third love attitude that helps us grow in our relationship. We learn this attitude from Christ in the Eucharist. At Mass we hear his word, we remember his sacrifice, and we receive him at communion. He gives us the graces we need to fill our life with generosity.

PRAYER

Jesus, gift of love to us from the Father,
you are our perfect model of generosity.
You willingly gave your life so that we might live.
We find ourselves often inattentive to each other's needs
and miss opportunities to give the other what is most needed.

We offer you our jar of generosity,
and ask you to bless us and fill our marriage
with selfless and joyful acts of kindness.

Help us to be aware of each other's needs,
responding even when it is difficult,

recognizing that our loving actions give the other a
tiny glimpse of your love
and knowing that what we share is a gift from you.

Amen.

Together recite the Hail Mary, the Memorare, and the Glory Be (these prayers can be found on pages 10–11).

PERSONAL/COUPLE REFLECTION

1. What are some examples of your spouse's generosity? Identify at least three.

2. What are the situations in which you enjoy the company of your spouse the most? Identify at least three.

3. What are some of the fun activities you like to do together? Identify at least three.

4. What do you believe is the benefit of having meals together?

5. How often do you have meals together? How do you feel about the frequency?

6. In what moments or situations of your day are electronic tools most likely to interfere with your being present to your spouse or your children?

7. Do you attend Mass regularly? If not, what keeps you?

GROUP SHARING

1. What stood out to you in this chapter that made you pause and think?

2. Do you understand what the authors mean when they draw a parallel between Christ's covenant, which we celebrate in the Mass, and the wedding covenant of husband and wife?

3. What are some examples of generosity and self-sacrifice that you have observed in your family or in couples you know?

4. What are your thoughts about couples spending time alone together, like regular date nights? How often do you go on a date or spend time alone together?

5. What are your thoughts about family meals and their frequency?

6. In your opinion, what are the benefits of frequent meals together?

7. Could you imagine a marriage in which spouses never ate together? What would it look like?

8. What advice about generosity would you give a newly married couple?

PRACTICE

This week schedule a time to do something fun together.
Or, for a week, plan one meal each day uninterrupted by any digital device.

Chapter 6

THE FOURTH JAR OF LOVE
Love Forgives

Please forgive me.

Married love is forgiving.
It is repairing the intimate bridges
damaged by our imperfections and selfishness.

* * *

Just as in the sacrament of penance and reconciliation
Christ shows us mercy, forgives our sins,
and heals our relationship with the Father and the Church,
in marriage husband and wife show mercy toward each other,
forgive one another's faults
and heal their relationship.

* * *

When husband and wife reconcile,
their forgiveness manifests God's merciful love.

Do you find it difficult to say, "I am sorry"? Most people do. Saying "I'm sorry" is admitting to another person that we are not perfect and we have failed. On the other hand, to say: "I forgive you" is also hard, because it feels like we are dismissing the pain caused us by our spouse.

The Holy Spirit Visited Us at Dairy Queen

A few years ago, I met with a couple who shared with me their story of forgiveness. After one year of stressful separation, and just one court date away from making the divorce final, Tom recalls: "I picked up the phone and called Pat. 'Pat, it's me,' I said. 'I just want to talk...As you know, our lawyers are sucking us dry. I would like for us, just you and me, to meet and agree among ourselves on how to settle our affairs...We need to stop the financial bleeding! Can you please meet me at Dairy Queen?'"

Sitting side-by-side in their living room and holding hands, Pat and Tom were telling me how they saved their marriage in spite of being on the verge of divorce. It all hinged on forgiveness. "The Holy Spirit visited us at Dairy Queen," says Pat with a smile. "I went there feeling very skeptical, distrustful, and afraid. I wasn't expecting anything new to happen. During the two hours that I sat across from Tom I was asking myself: 'What am I doing here? Is this a mistake?' Yet I also felt a certain sense of comfort. There were moments when I felt like we had never left each other."

Tom added, "That day we left Dairy Queen not sure of what would come next. However, that meeting led to other meetings and eventually to rediscovering the 'us' that we had lost. What helped us most was a special program we saw advertised in the parish bulletin. The name of the program is "Retrouvaille."

Retrouvaille is a French word that means "rediscovery." It is a peer ministry, offered specifically to help hurting couples, even those already separated or divorced, to recover their marriage.

Pat continued: "I went to the Retrouvaille weekend still very resistant and distrustful of Tom. I had been hurt badly and was not willing to make myself vulnerable and risk being hurt again. It was not until the Saturday of that weekend that I finally realized that I had to make a decision. I had to choose to either stay hurt or to start healing. I had to choose to let go and forgive or to hold on to mistrust and bitterness. I decided I wanted to heal. I chose recovery. I chose forgiveness."(Learn more about Retrouvaille at www.helpourmarriage.org.)

"The weak can never forgive. Forgiveness is the attribute of the strong."
■ **MAHATMA GANDHI**

Forgiveness is the love attitude contained in the fourth jar of love. According to social researchers, the presence of the attitude of forgiveness has been linked to better conflict resolution,[44] and therefore stronger marriages. We learn how to forgive from Christ, in the confessional. Consider what happens when we go to confession.

The Sacrament of Penance and Reconciliation

Jesus Christ established the sacrament of reconciliation so that we can experience the mercifulness of the Father. After his resurrection, Jesus appeared to the disciples and breathed on them, saying, "Receive the Holy Spirit. If you forgive the sins of any, they are forgiven them; if you retain the sins of any, they are retained" (John 20:22–23). He gave the apostles the power to forgive sins. Today, the priest, through the sacrament of holy orders and as a representative of Christ, exercises this power in the sacrament of reconciliation. Through this sacrament, Christ, the Bridegroom, reconciles us, members of the Church, his Bride, with the Father. Through confession we experience God's mercy, and we leave the confessional at peace with God and the world.

"Confession is an act of honesty and courage, an act of entrusting ourselves, beyond sin, to the mercy of a loving and forgiving father."
■ **ST. JOHN PAUL II, 1987, SAN ANTONIO**

The Prodigal Son

Many say that in today's culture we do not appreciate the power and value of forgiveness because we have forgotten what "sin" is. We learn in the Bible that sin is a disobedience to God (Deuteronomy 9:7). It is a selfish act of turning away from God, a declaration of independence, as Adam and Eve did in the Garden of Eden. They wanted to be like God. They ignored God's will to do their own, and we all know how that turned out. Sins come in many shades and colors. Their gravity varies depending on the seriousness of the disobedience. God forgives all, big and small.

Jesus gave us a picture of sin and of God's mercy in the parable of the prodigal son (Luke 15:11–32). This is the story of a rebellious son who was intent on pursuing his own dreams and said to his father, "Give me my inheritance now." This was an impertinent request. The son cared only about himself and had no concern for how his request might hurt his father and his brother. In spite of this, the father agreed. A few days later the son turned his back on his father and older brother and headed out to pursue his dreams. He left to chart a course for his own life away from home, independent of his father and disconnected from his family. However, the path chosen did not turn out to be what he expected. He soon squandered all his fortune and was penniless.

Desperate, he accepted a job tending pigs and was so hungry that he wished he could eat the food the pigs were served. Life away from the father was miserable, and he started remembering the good life at his father's home. He realized that even the servants there did not go hungry. To avoid starving, he decided to go back. So he left to return home.

Meanwhile, the father had been missing his son so much that he would look in the distance for him often. One day he spotted his son returning home and "was filled with compassion," Jesus tells us. He ran toward the son and embraced him and kissed him. He said to his servants, "Let us eat and celebrate; for this son of mine was dead and is alive again; he was lost and is found!" (Luke 15:20–24).

All of us are like the prodigal son. We want independence. We often turn our back on those we love; we disconnect. We sin and stray away from home. But God wants us to be with him, and he waits for us like the father in the parable. There comes a point when our sin catches up and causes us pain. Returning home is what we desire deep in our heart, and it is what God desires for us. Confession is the sacrament that gives us the Father's loving embrace welcoming us back home.

This pattern of sin, repentance, forgiveness, and reconciliation, which we see in Jesus' parable, is the dynamic we live not only in our relationship with God but also in our relationship with our spouse. We can all learn from the father to be merciful toward each other. Without forgiveness our relationships deteriorate very quickly.

"Be kind to one another, compassionate, forgiving one another for God has forgiven you in Christ." ▪ **EPHESIANS 4:32**

Forgiveness: An Everyday Attitude

Forgiveness is an attitude we need to repair major injuries in our relationships and to heal the small daily bruises we suffer in our interactions. Martin Luther King Jr. said: "Forgiveness is not an occasional act, it is a constant attitude." We are imperfect, and sometimes in our daily encounters we hurt one another, often unintentionally; we say a word or do something that offends our spouse or causes a misunderstanding; we forget a promise made and bring pain to the relationship. Think about your activities in the past few days. Has your spouse said something or done something that hurt your feelings or made you uncomfortable? Or have you done something or said something that caused a misunderstanding with your spouse or your children? Often we cause each other pain unintentionally, yet it takes forgiveness to heal the tension created by our shortcomings or inadvertent missteps in our daily life.

We asked couples we know: What are some of the interactions with your spouse that cause both of you to feel pain? Here are some of their responses.

- "When I don't try to consider his point of view."

- "It's the bills. Money is an issue for us. We argue a lot about money. I'm a spender; she's a saver."

- "I'm a big football fan, and before I got married, I liked to sit down and watch a few games on the weekend, but since our wedding my wife doesn't understand why I waste time like that."

- "I cause pain to my spouse by being inattentive. I'm too wrapped up in what I'm doing and what I want."

- "By putting my career before him and the family sometimes."

- "By not standing by his side in particular situations."

- "My moodiness causes my spouse discomfort because when something is bothering me I tend to shut down and not say anything, and my wife wonders what's wrong."

These are some of the imperfections, some of our humanness, that we bring to the relationship when we marry, and unfortunately from time to time we hurt each other with them. Forgiveness is like the oil that we can pour on our wounds to soothe the raw spots.

The Wedding Bread

Because of our imperfections, our daily life is dotted with small encounters that sometimes leave a bad taste in our mouth. I (John) am reminded of a conversation I had years ago with my tour guide in Russia. I was in Moscow on a business trip, and I was touring the Kremlin. While walking through Red Square and inside the Kremlin I saw several wedding parties posing for pictures. I asked my tour guide, Olga, to tell me some Russian wedding customs. She told me about the Russian wedding bread.

She said that on the day before the wedding the mother of the bride prepares a special loaf of bread for the new couple. The bread is sweet, and the mother sprinkles it generously with salt. The bread is eaten during the meal following the wedding. Olga explained that the loaf symbolizes married life. Some of it is sweet and some of it is bitter. While salt is a symbol of permanence, its taste clashes with the sweetness of the bread. It represents the discomfort we are causing each other each day, most often unintentionally. Do you experience "the taste of salt" in your marriage from time to time? When was the last time?

Without forgiveness, which helps us overlook some of our spouse's shortcomings, we can easily grow in resentment. Italian psychologist Roberto Asagioli wrote that life without forgiveness is an endless cycle of resentment and retaliation.

"Resentment is like drinking poison and then hoping it will kill your enemies." ■ **NELSON MANDELA**

An Ounce of Prevention Is Worth a Pound of Cure (Benjamin Franklin)

It is important to ask forgiveness for our failings, but it is far better to prevent the failing so that we do not hurt our spouse. Benjamin Franklin's axiom reminds us of this. During a visit with my sister and brother-in-law, who live in Italy, I found each of them complaining to me about the other. She was saying: "Retired life would be great if he was not so stubborn. When he sets his mind to do something he does it, and either I go along with it or we fight. The house is a mess. He starts a project, then another, then one more, and never finishes any one of them. His presence at home twenty-four hours a day drives me crazy."

I heard a similar litany from her husband: "I retired first and I had my own comfortable routine at home during the day. Now she is at home, and we get in each other's way. She criticizes everything I do, including my favorite hobbies. For years I enjoyed tending to our garden. When she was working she had no interest in it. Now she is telling me what to plant and when to plant it, and she calls my garden a jungle."

"Forgiveness is not about forgetting. It is about letting go of another person's throat." ■ **WILLIAM PAUL YOUNG, AUTHOR OF** *THE SHACK*

What we learned during our forty-five years of marriage and from listening to couples is that complaining to other people about our spouse, as my sister and brother-in-law were in the habit of doing, does not ease a couple's stress. On the contrary, it aggravates the situation and erodes the bond of the relationship. Through their complaining, the spouses reinforce in their own minds what bothers them about the other and sustain their hostility for future battles.

An ounce of prevention in this case would mean to refrain from complaining to others about our disagreements as a couple; it could also mean to look at the situation from a different perspective, a more positive outlook, one that eases the friction.

Mercy and Gratefulness

As we mentioned earlier, Dr. John Gottman's research tells us that sixty-nine percent of marital conflicts cannot be resolved and are recurring. Marriage is a contact sport. We cannot go through our days without bumping into each other with differences of opinions, habits that grate on us, or words that unintentionally offend or cause a misunderstanding. Each day in our life as a married couple we may have exchanges that can cause minor scrapes and bruises.

Rather than dwell on the discomfort or brood over the last thing our spouse said or did that bothered us, we encourage couples to stand back and look at their spouse and their marriage with an attitude of mercy and gratefulness.

I (Teri) remember a moment, years ago, when I had an insight while cleaning the bathroom. Each day as I cleaned the sinks I would notice drops of shaving cream left by John earlier that morning. I would become annoyed and I would say to myself: "Why can't he clean up after himself?" One day, when John was out of town for a business trip, I noticed that his sink remained clean. I missed John and realized that I would rather see a messy sink—a sign that he is home—and feel gratefulness, than be aggravated by the shaving cream in the sink. Gratefulness, which is an aspect of generosity, is an important attitude in life; one that helps us see life from a different perspective, a positive one.

In our home we have a sign that reads: Gratitude turns what we have into enough.

Four Behaviors that Empty Our Jars

Social scientists encourage us to avoid four specific behaviors that can disconnect us from our spouse: criticism, contempt, defensiveness, and stonewalling. Dr. John Gottman calls these the Four Horsemen of the Apocalypse[45] because they are deadly to the marriage.

> *Criticism* is a message that accuses or blames and attacks our spouse's character: "We are always late because of you!" "You never do your part!" "You're lazy."
>
> *Contempt* is an outright insult with the intent of causing hurt:

"One has to be dumb to do such a thing." "You don't know what you're talking about." Often sarcasm is an expression of contempt.

Defensiveness is a counterattack mounted by the spouse that has been injured by criticism or contempt; it contains the same venom, and possibly in a higher dosage.

Stonewalling is turning our back on our spouse and disconnecting, often expressed with a behavior that some call the "silent treatment." This behavior sends a message that says, "You are invisible to me." "You are insignificant." "Whatever you say or do is not affecting me."

According to Dr. Gottman, some of these four behaviors are likely to appear in any marriage. However, they become particularly dangerous to the couple when they turn into habits.

As you might notice, these behaviors tend to build on one another and are damaging to the marriage. Perhaps we learned these behaviors when we were growing up and they have become habits that hold us back in our relationship.

To make progress on your journey to reconnect with each other we encourage you to take a first step: eliminate *criticism* from your interactions. Find ways to express your disagreement, disappointment, or hurts without demeaning each other, such as: "Can we agree to disagree?" "I really feel bad when we are late at functions." "I did not know you felt that way."

If what triggers the critical remarks is a recurring conflict with your spouse, address the conflict calmly. We believe that if you can stop criticizing each other you will make progress in keeping contempt, defensiveness, and stonewalling from taking up residence in your relationship.

Take a moment to reflect:

- What situations in your relationship lead you to criticize your spouse?

- Can you imagine interacting with your spouse in these situations without being critical, blaming, or accusing? Would you consider simply describing how you feel when your spouse says or does something that hurts you?

How to Ask Forgiveness

Asking forgiveness requires humility because we have to admit our imperfections and our faults. The following are some points to remember when asking forgiveness.

1. When you realize that something you said or did has hurt your spouse, and you feel sorry, pause and ask for God's forgiveness. Even if the hurt you caused was unintentional, as it often is, you have hurt one of God's children. This is also a time to ask God for guidance on how to approach your spouse with words that express your sorrow.

2. Then approach your spouse. Too often we say "I'm sorry" as if that is enough to repair the damage done. However, it helps the process of healing if we are specific about our regrets. For example: "I should not have said…. I am very sorry. It was an impulsive act and I regret doing it. Will you please forgive me?"

3. Promise that you will do your best to not repeat the mistake.

4. If your spouse wants to tell you how he/she feels, listen attentively. Your spouse wants you to know their pain. Listening is part of your penance.

5. Some of us say "I'm sorry" expecting to move forward as if nothing has happened. The fact is healing takes time. Be patient with your spouse's rate of recovery and healing. Don't hurt your spouse further by saying something like: "Are you still upset? Why don't you get over it?"

Sorrow for our faults and forgiveness are aspects of an attitude that nurtures love in our marriage relationship. This attitude reconnects spouses and heals what is broken.

"Forgiveness says you are given another chance to make a new beginning." ■ **DESMOND TUTU**

The attitude of forgiveness is something we need to develop in our marriage if we want our relationship to last. We are all imperfect, and we all need forgiveness from time to time. Forgiveness is a quality of love that we learn from Jesus, and in him we find the strength to forgive our spouse or to ask for forgiveness. Making use of confession is a great way to receive the graces that help us become better persons and rebuild broken relationships. We all make mistakes because we are not perfect. Forgiveness is an everyday attitude that soothes the friction that can occur in our daily interactions.

PRAYER

Merciful Jesus, we, your prodigal children, come to you.
Too often we turn our backs on you and on each other,
and we allow our selfish behaviors to come between us.

Filled with sorrow and contrition,
we ask you to heal our hearts with your mercy and forgiveness.

We offer you our jar of forgiveness and ask you
to bless us and fill our marriage
with loving words and gestures of contrition and sorrow.
Help us turn to you when we are disconnected
by the pain of a disagreement or the sting of an insult.
Guide us to return to each other,
knowing that the love that we share is a gift from you.

Amen.

Together recite the Hail Mary, the Memorare, and the Glory Be (these prayers can be found on pages 10–11).

PERSONAL/COUPLE REFLECTION

Take a few moments to reflect on the following questions and then share your thoughts with your spouse.

1. When was the last time you did or said something that hurt your spouse?

2. What is your typical way of saying to your spouse that you are sorry and want forgiveness? Have you ever wondered how your spouse feels about the way you say that you are sorry? We encourage you to ask.

3. What can you learn from the parable of the Prodigal Son that applies to you?

4. What are the typical interactions that cause friction between you and your spouse? Identify two situations in which you are likely to clash. What can you do to smooth your interactions in these situations?

5. Is criticism something you or your spouse use with each other from time to time? What can you do to change that behavior?

6. Are contempt or sarcasm present in your relationship? Reflect on your experience of sarcastic remarks directed at you, and how they hurt.

7. Is the silent treatment a behavior that is present in your relationship? What can you do to reconnect?

8. Gratitude is the antidote to the discontent that can erode our relationship. Name three qualities of your spouse for which you are grateful.

Do not forget to turn to Mary and Jesus for help in filling your fourth jar of love with forgiveness.

GROUP SHARING

1. Have any of the Four Horsemen appeared in your marriage?
   Which ones? How do you handle them?

2. When you and your spouse have a hurtful disagreement,
   how do you heal your relationship? Does it take one of you
   longer than the other to get over the hurt? How do you find
   your way back to each other?

3. What do you know about Retrouvaille?

4. When you are angry or disappointed with your spouse how
   can you avoid using criticism to express your feelings? What
   words can you use to tell how you feel without humiliating
   your spouse?

5. As a group, define the word "sarcasm." Is sarcasm present
   in some of your interactions? What are you trying to
   accomplish with your sarcastic remarks? What are other
   ways to make your point that show respect for your spouse?

6. If you are caught up in a conflict that causes you to retreat
   and give each other the "silent treatment," how do you
   break up the stalemate? Share ideas of how different couples
   approach these situations.

7. In your opinion, what are the benefits of gratitude?

Chapter 7

THE FIFTH JAR OF LOVE
Love Is Compassionate

"In sickness and in health…"

Married love heals.
Spouses accompany each other
with compassion and understanding
during moments of pain.

* * *

Just as in the sacrament of anointing of the sick
Christ shows God's compassion by forgiving and comforting us,
in marriage husband and wife protect
each other's vulnerable sides
and give each other comfort in moments of pain
out of compassion.

* * *

When husband and wife show tender loving care for each other,
their love manifests Christ's compassionate love for his Bride,
the Church.

It was a dreary and rainy February day, and I (John) was in bed and in a lot of pain. I could not make any move because any change in my body's position would send shocks waves of pain from my lower back across my body. I had a serious case of sciatica. One of my spinal disks was pressing on a nerve and causing not only excruciating pain but also numbness in my right leg and foot. I was scheduled for surgery, but it was not imminent, and Teri was concerned because the medications I was taking were only partially effective in relieving the pain. Wanting to be of help, she said, "I would like to call Fr. Kibby and ask if I can take you to church to receive the anointing of the sick. That may give you some relief." I protested, thinking I was not feeling bad enough to receive the sacrament, but she called anyway. Father was very kind and told her to come to the parish. Teri helped me in the car and drove me to church, trying to avoid any bumps on the road that could cause me more pain. When we arrived at the church Fr. Kibby, our pastor, was waiting. He could tell I was in a lot of pain and asked where I would be most comfortable. I sat in a pew in the back of the church, and he sat across from me and began the prayers of the rite. Father explained that this was like going to confession, so we said the act of contrition (*confiteor*), and then he anointed my forehead and my hands with the blessed oil. What I found very consoling and encouraging were the words of the prayer that followed: "Father in heaven, through this holy anointing grant John comfort in his suffering. When he is afraid, give him courage. When afflicted, give him patience, when dejected, afford him hope, and when alone, assure him of the support of your holy people. We ask this through Christ our Lord. Amen."

That day I left our parish church not feeling physically better but with my spirit lifted; I was in a positive mental state, which helped me bear the pain. I was grateful that Teri had arranged for me to receive this sacrament, and I felt strengthened by the knowledge that God and the Church were close to me, praying with me during my days of suffering.

The Fifth Jar of Love: Compassion

In this chapter we reflect on the fifth jar of love: the attitude of compassion, a quality in our love that makes our relationship warm and comforting, a place where our spouse can help us heal the wounds that life inflicts. We learn this healing attitude from God, who said to his people in the Old Testament: "The Lord longs to be gracious to you, therefore he will rise up to show you compassion" (Isaiah 30:18). In the New Testament Christ manifested the Father's compassion to the people he healed, and today we feel God's compassion and comfort in our encounter with Jesus in the sacrament of anointing of the sick.

The Sacrament of Anointing of the Sick

The sacrament of anointing of the sick was instituted by Christ and is prescribed by St. James: "Is anyone among you sick? Let him call the presbyters of the church, and let them pray over him, anointing him with oil in the name of the Lord" (James 5:14).

This sacrament is for everyone who is sick. It is encouraged specifically prior to a serious operation, during a pregnancy, or when an elderly person's frailty is becoming more pronounced. The sacrament can only be administered by a priest who in prayer lays his hands on the head of the sick person and then anoints the forehead and the hands.

*"As a father has compassion on his children,
so the Lord has compassion on those who fear him."*
■ **PSALM 103:13**

On the day I received the anointing of the sick I felt that God was present, the whole Church was praying with me, and my suffering had meaning. One of the prayers I heard was: "Lord…since you have given John a share in your own passion, help him find hope in suffering…" Our suffering allows us to join Christ in his passion, for our salvation and the salvation of others.

This sacrament is an act of compassionate love through which Christ comforts his Bride, the Church. Compassion is a quality of spousal love that helps us heal and grow as a couple.

Married Love Is Healing

A few years ago the *New York Times* tried to grab its readers' attention with the headline: "Is Marriage Good for your Health?" The author, Tara-Parker Pope, reviewed the science behind the claim that marriage is good for our health. She reported numerous studies starting as far back as 1858 that show how marriage is beneficial to the health of the spouses. She noted that, over time, as research methods became more sophisticated, we learned that it is not enough to be married to benefit emotionally and physically from marriage; it is the quality of the relationship that makes a difference. Time and again, it is proven that the closer the spouses are to each other, the better their immune system functions and the faster their wounds heal. Scientists report that couples in strong marriages are healthier and live longer.

Helping Each Other Carry Our Crosses

In moments of sickness it is a blessing to have someone next to us who is helping us to carry our cross. Wendy and Chuck are a couple who do this with grace. We see them at Mass every Sunday. They stand out to us because of the way they interact with each other. There are times when Wendy wears dark glasses and is unstable on her feet, and Chuck is always attentive and close by to give her support and to guide her.

Wendy was diagnosed in 2015 with a form of MS that causes her to have serious symptoms from time to time when the disease flares up. The condition has affected her ability to function by attacking her senses: "Lights bother me, and sounds hurt my ears. I lost the sense of taste and smell." Her memory has also been affected. This limits what she can do. She depends on others to drive her to places, to cook, to shop, to pay bills, and to do the main chores that she used to do. Most of this falls on Chuck now.

Wendy loves her husband and two sons and does not like the way her condition is affecting them: "I am mostly upset for the stress that I put on the people around me. When I was first diagnosed, I thought: just put me in a cave and go about living your life. I will come out when I feel better." Wendy is a very energetic person and does not like to feel helpless.

Chuck comments: "Our world has been turned upside down. Even the dogs sense that something is wrong with Wendy and keep checking on her."

All of this is a heavy load for Chuck to carry. We asked him how he copes. "My first loyalty is to Wendy. Her condition demands a lot of me, and I give willingly because I love her. It is my love for Wendy that gives me the strength to carry on. A few years ago, I even declined a promotion at work because it would add more responsibility. Wendy is my priority."

Chuck and Wendy have been married thirty years and recently had their marriage blessed in the Church. Chuck is a convert to the Catholic faith. He says: "We feel more at peace now. Being married in the Church is something we talked about for a long time." He added that he finds comfort in going to Mass. "We go to Mass regularly. Church is a place where I feel safe. It feels good to be around people we know and who care for us."

In observing how Chuck helps Wendy we are reminded of the mysterious figure from the gospel's passion narrative: Simon of Cyrene. He did not volunteer to carry Jesus' cross but accepted with grace a task forced upon him. He is a model for all of us.

The Bride without Shoes

It was the day after our wedding, and I (John) remember our drive on Interstate 70 going east, away from Kansas City toward the Lake of the Ozarks in Missouri. It was a snowy and windy November day. But inside our little car, a 1970 orange Maverick, it was warm and cozy. It was the place where we wanted to be. It was our car. It represented our new world. It was just the two of us, starting our life together. We had dreamed of spending our honeymoon strolling the Ozarks hills and visiting many quaint places. The snow that was coming down, wet and heavy, was redesigning our plans. That did not bother us. What was important to us was that we were together. It snowed for two days. On the third day, although there were ten inches of snow on the ground, we decided to get out to explore the area.

As we were leaving our hotel, I realized that Teri did not bring shoes that I thought were appropriate for walking in the snow.

She was wearing dress shoes. So, wanting to exert my newly acquired role and responsibility of "provider," I said to Teri, "Let's go buy you a pair of boots." So off we went in the car looking for a place to buy boots.

At the nearby town we found a shoe store. I got out of the car and stood in the street, ankle deep in snow. I wondered how Teri would get to the store through piles of slush and mud without getting wet and dirty. Then I had an idea. I walked to the passenger side of the car, opened the door, and picked Teri up in my arms. There I was, at the center of town, carrying my beautiful bride to buy her boots. I carried her all the way inside the store while bystanders who had noticed what was happening started clapping.

That was a gallant gesture that impressed my young bride, and it has remained a vivid memory in Teri's mind. In fact, from time to time she reminds me of what I did and asks when I am going to carry her again with so much enthusiasm.

Spouses that want to succeed need to learn to carry each other's burdens. Teri carried me when I was sick; she looked after my needs and helped me recuperate after surgery. She carried me when I was mourning the loss of a job and supported me for six months while I was looking for another job. I have done the same for her many times.

A spouse is the friend and companion who supports us when we encounter a dark cloud, holds our hand and cares for us when we feel down, keeps track of our medicine when we are confused, and feeds us when we cannot serve ourselves. That is why marriage is good for our health.[46] Linda Waite and Maggie Gallagher, in their book *The Case for Marriage*, write that married people, because of what they do for each other, are healthier, happier, and better off financially.[47]

Can you remember a time when you were sick or felt a lot of stress and your spouse's care and attention lifted you up?

Protecting Each Other's Vulnerable Sides

There is a book called *How to Improve Your Marriage Without Talking About It* by Patricia Love and Steven Stosny.[48] When I first learned about it I (John) was intrigued by the title. I knew from my experience as a marriage counselor that all couples want to improve their marriage, and definitely most husbands would like to do so without talking about it. They would like to just get their toolbox and fix it without going through the agony of feeling inadequate in trying to express verbally how they feel.

Patricia Love and Steven Stosny explain that both men and women aspire to experience a strong emotional bond with their spouse. However, because men and women are different they will arrive at the experience of being connected in different ways. Normally, to feel better connected, women want to talk about the relationship. On the other hand talking does not make men feel better. The outcome is that both men and women may end up frustrated. Love and Stosny suggest that the answer is not in teaching men to talk, but in helping both men and women become aware of each other's needs and to act as protector of one another's vulnerabilities.

Mary, our niece, and Tanner, her husband, have been married four years and are a great example to us of how spouses work together to protect one another's vulnerable sides. Mary has dyslexia and finds it hard to read. We learned recently that in the evenings she and Tanner read books together. Tanner reads out loud to her so she does not have to struggle reading. She is grateful for Tanner's compassion and care. This caring gesture keeps them connected and their relationship is strengthened by it.

Stu and Lisa—Working as a Team

There is another aspect of the healing power of spousal love. Sometimes one spouse may need to take a strong stand to pull the other out of the "ditch." This is necessary when a person's poor habits affect not only oneself but the relationship. To save the marriage, the loving spouse may need to actively intervene.

We visited Stu and Lisa in their home to record their story for one of our videos. Stu, sitting next to Lisa, admitted to his addiction to pornography and recounted how it started. "I started using pornography during my teen years when I discovered a stack of *Playboy* magazines that belonged to my parents," said Stu. "No one told me that pornography was wrong. It was only when Lisa came into my life, during my college years, that she objected, and when our conversation turned toward marriage, Lisa told me that pornography was not something she wanted in our relationship."

Seeking Lisa's love, Stu complied and got rid of his collection of magazines and videos. "It was at that point that I realized that I was addicted to pornography and the temptations were strong," said Stu.

Lisa explained that in the early years of their marriage, when Stu had a setback she would get upset, because she thought that Stu did not find her desirable. But one day she realized that Stu was not rejecting her as a woman for pornography. He was possessed by a craving like that of a person who is addicted to alcohol or drugs. "So, instead of being mad at Stu, I became mad at the addiction, our common enemy, the enemy of our marriage," said Lisa. "The addiction was something we had to fight against, together as a team."

And so they did! They started by turning to God in prayer for strength. The addiction, like any other, does not go away, but they are fighting it together.

Lisa is helping Stu manage his condition by encouraging him to belong to a support group that holds Stu accountable for his choices.

Sometimes We Fail but Faith Can Help

In married life and family life, nothing ever stays the same, but sometimes the transitions are drastic, sudden, and unexpected. Such changes are often brought on by illnesses, accidents, job losses, relocations, and many others. Those are moments where we find ourselves mourning what we have lost or left behind, and all we can do is console each other as we move forward. That is difficult when both are grieving, and sometimes we fall short.

For us, one of these experiences happened with the loss of my (John) job and having to relocate our family to a distant city to pursue a new career opportunity. I recall traveling with Teri to the new town to buy a home and noticing Teri's emotions going up and down as the days passed. When we first arrived Teri was excited about the new place, a small town. Seeing all the white picket fences, she remarked: "This is a *Leave It to Beaver* type of town." Then reality set in. There were five homes from which we could choose. This was followed by feelings of depression for not being able to imagine our family living in a small town and missing all our friends back home. Teri cried a lot in the privacy of our hotel room. She was grieving. To make the move Teri had to resign from her position as Director of Adult Formation at our parish. She also felt the pain of moving our younger daughter, who had just finished her freshman year in high school. In those moments I felt helpless in comforting her.

To be honest, I was not very supportive. When Teri expressed her disappointment with the situation I would get defensive and then angry and frustrated. I felt backed into a corner. On the one hand I did not want our family to move because of the pain this event was causing. On the other hand, our financial reserves were running short. I needed a job to provide for the needs of our family. We were all mourning, and it was difficult to help each other because I too was grieving.

Fortunately our faith helped us through this moment of transition. It helped us keep our life in perspective—to realize that our options were limited and to accept the opportunity we were being offered. We trusted that God had a reason for our being in that place at that time. This was a passage in our life that we needed to go through and to grow because of it with the help of God's grace. I (Teri) found comfort in the words of Peter at the Transfiguration: "Lord, it is good for us to be here" (Matthew 17:4). I would repeat it often during the day, and it has become a mantra for the times when we face changes or challenges in our life. After John retired, when we were building a new home, I wrote the passage on one of the studs over the sink in the kitchen before the drywall was installed. Often the task of washing the dishes is a reflective time for me.

In retrospect that adversity was a life lesson that helped us as a couple and as a family. We found support in the local community and met very many kind people. We remember fondly the year we were there, because that experience impacted our life positively. We thank God for the experience.

The memories of those days continue to bring comfort to me

(Teri). Throughout my life, when I have needed to solve a problem I found myself at my grandmother's house in my dreams at night. Since the move, I find myself at the house where we lived for one year in that small loving community. That is now the place where I go to solve my problems in my dreams.

We Carry Our Crosses With Christ

As we learn from the rite of the anointing of the sick, our pains and sufferings are a share in Christ's passion. Knowing this does not make our sorrows less heavy, but our faith gives meaning to our experience and gives us the knowledge that we are not alone. We are with Christ on his way to Calvary. He gives us the graces we need to carry our cross with the help of our spouse.

"There is no cross, big or small, in our life which the Lord does not share with us." ■ **POPE FRANCIS**[49]

As husband and wife we can help each other like Simon the Cyrenian (Luke 23:26) helped Jesus carry his cross on the way to Calvary. He relieved Jesus' shoulders of a terrible burden and eased his pain. Spouses do the same for each other in many different ways, and sometimes a reassuring smile or a gentle touch are enough to lift a heavy burden because they say: "I am right beside you!" Our spouse's love is a reminder of God's compassion.

Touch has the power to ease our pain. Tara Parker-Pope[50] reports in her book *For Better* about the benefits of hand holding by spouses. She cites a study that found that when a husband holds his wife's hand, he is doing more than just showing affection. He is lowering his wife's stress level.

Hold hands as often as possible!

PRAYER

Compassionate Jesus,
you made the blind see and the deaf hear.
Time and again you cured the suffering that crossed your path
begging for your mercy and healing.
We too are in need of your mercy and graces.

We offer you our jar of compassion and ask you
to bless us and fill our marriage
with heartfelt tenderness for each other.
Transform our words and actions into holy medicine,
soothing the mind and body of our beloved spouse.

Help us to remember that you are present
in our most vulnerable times,
fully aware that the love that we share is a gift from you.

Amen.

Together recite the Hail Mary, the Memorare, and the Glory Be (these prayers can be found on pages 10–11).

PERSONAL/COUPLE REFLECTION

1. What have been the low points in your love story?

2. Recall a particular difficult moment and ask yourself: "How did I help my spouse through it?" or "How did my spouse help me through it?"

3. What are your vulnerable sides that you need your spouse to protect? Does he/she know what they are? If he/she does not know, are you willing to reveal your vulnerable sides to your spouse?

4. What is something that you can do today for your spouse that would help him/her feel understood and cared for by you?

5. Do you and your spouse hold hands? How have you experienced the healing power of your spouse's touch?

GROUP SHARING

1. Who are some of the couples in your life that have been models of compassion in the way they helped each other through tough times?

2. In your opinion what did the couples that you identified in the previous question do for each other that helped them get through the tough times? *caregivers*

3. How would you define the quality of love we call "compassion"? When does your spouse show compassion?

4. How or when have you experienced the soothing and
   healing power of a kind word or touch from your spouse?
   Give some examples.

ACTION

During the coming week be aware of your spouse's needs. Hold
hands whenever possible.

Chapter 8

THE SIXTH JAR OF LOVE
Love Serves

It's not about us.

Married love is servant love.
Spouses accept a vocation to serve.
They serve God, they serve one another, and they serve society.

* * *

Just as in the sacrament of holy orders and matrimony
Christ serves his Bride, the Church,
in the marriage relationship husband and wife serve each other,
and together they serve God, with the help of Christ's grace.

* * *

When husband and wife serve God and each other,
their love fulfills their vocation and gives glory to God,
and they find joy.

SHORTLY AFTER TERI AND I WERE ENGAGED AND WE LIVED IN KANSAS CITY, I RECEIVED A LETTER IN THE MAIL FROM THE ITALIAN SELECTIVE SERVICE ASKING ME TO RETURN TO ITALY TO REPORT FOR MY MANDATORY MILITARY SERVICE. In other words, I was drafted. That note came as a surprise. At first, I thought it was a joke, but then the reality sank in. I was an Italian citizen, and it was my duty to serve. While studying in the United States I had been given a deferment because I was a student. Now it was my turn to be enlisted.

At that point in my life I had decided that my future would be in the United States. I had applied for permanent residence status. I had a job and now a fiancée with plans to marry in a few months. I did not want to leave for an undetermined time, perhaps two years, to serve in the Italian military.

What complicated my situation was the fact that when I applied for permanent residence status, I was told that the process of receiving a green card might take up to two years, and in the meantime I could not leave the United States for any reason; otherwise, I could not return until the day my turn came to receive the green card.

Thinking about my choices was depressing. On the one hand I could ignore the request from the Italian military and continue my life in the United States, and be considered a draft dodger in my country, Italy. On the other, I could go to Italy and serve, and not know when I would be allowed to return to the United States.

I spent several agonizing months talking to the Italian Consulate in St. Louis, and to the United States Immigration Department in Kansas City, where I lived, all to no avail. The choice was mine. Finally, Teri and I, taking the long view on life, decided that since I was still an Italian citizen, I owed it to my country to serve. So, I left for Italy to enlist in the military service on May 1, 1972.

Fortunately, once I arrived in Italy and reported to the Army post, after many tests and exams, I was dismissed and exonerated from service. That was great news, however, I still could not return to the United States. So, I started working with the American Consulate in Italy to arrange for a visa. It took a few months but thankfully, by September of the same year, I was back in Kansas City, at my job and with Teri. We married in November.

We are all called to serve because we are members of and belong to a community. In our communities we depend on one another, and we exist as a society only because of each other's services. Service is an essential part of life and of any marriage relationship. The attitude of service is the good wine found in the sixth jar of love.

Jesus Is Our Model

We learn the meaning of service from Jesus, who at the Last Supper wanted to teach his disciples and us a lesson about serving. He, who was the teacher, bent down to wash his disciples' feet. Then he said: "Do you realize what I have done for you?… If I, the Master and teacher, have washed your feet, you ought to wash one another's feet. I have given you a model to follow, so that as I have done for you, you should do…If you understand this, blessed are you if you do it" (John 13:12, 15–17).

Today, Christ serves the Father and the Church through the special graces he gives those he calls to the priesthood and matrimony. Priesthood and marriage are vocations to serve others. In the Church there are other vocations, but Christ elevated these two to the level of sacrament because of their importance to the life of the Church.

Holy Orders and Matrimony

According to the *Catechism of the Catholic Church*, married couples and priests are "consecrated" to serve.[51] They receive these sacraments not for themselves but for others. Spouses receive the graces they need to carry out their duties toward God, each other, their children, and their neighbors. That is why this chapter is subtitled "It's not about us." Marriage is a call to serve others.

For us Christians, doing God's will as a married couple defines the purpose and direction for our life together, and it is the source of our joy.

"Joy is the infallible sign of the presence of God."
■ **TEILHARD DE CHARDIN**

Serving Our Domestic Church

Since the Second Vatican Council the Catholic Church has made reference to the Christian home as a "domestic church"[52] or the church of the home. While the priest serves God through his work in the parish community, husbands and wives serve God in their home. In their homes spouses are the priests, the teachers, and the leaders dedicated to serve.[53]

How do we serve? We could say that the services we perform in our homes is the practice of the Spiritual and Corporal Works of Mercy. The works of mercy are specific actions identified by the Church from the teachings of Jesus. By practicing them we follow Jesus' example of serving others.

In the *Catechism of the Catholic Church* we read that the works of mercy are charitable actions through which we help our neighbors. The Spiritual Works of Mercy are instructing, advising, consoling, comforting, forgiving, and bearing wrongs patiently. The Corporal Works of Mercy are feeding the hungry, sheltering the homeless, clothing the naked, visiting the sick and imprisoned, and burying the dead (CCC, 2447).

The Church reminds us that these are our duties toward our neighbors. Our first neighbors are the people who live under our roof, the members of our domestic church: our spouse, our children, our elderly parents, brothers and sisters, relatives, and so on. As you read the list of works of mercy, you may be able to see how each day you have the opportunity to practice them in what you do. In your domestic church you feed the hungry every day, you give shelter and clothing, and you take care of the sick. You teach, advise, console, comfort, and forgive, and hopefully you do all of this with great patience and joy.

We Serve to the End

The house is quiet, and the mid-afternoon sunlight coming through the big picture window hits the kitchen table that sits next to it and brightens the room, creating an intimate setting for our conversation. Jim is a young-looking eighty-seven-year-old with a full head of white hair and a friendly smile. He is eager to talk about the love of his life: his wife, Betty, to whom he has been married for sixty-five years. He is talking about her as if she were there sipping coffee with us. But Betty is not there. She is at a nearby assisted living facility because she is battling Alzheimer's disease. Jim visits her every day and brings her favorite treats. Jim's face lights up when he tells me how Betty, who is forgetting most things, still recognizes and remembers him.

He says: "She raises her arms and says out loud, 'Here comes my husband.'"

Jim serves Betty at this stage of their life when he visits her each day. He brings her out of the fog for a few precious moments, and together they recall some of the events in their sixty-five-year-old marriage and life with their children. They often revisit the same stories day after day because Betty does not remember the previous day's conversation.

What is asked of us, as followers of Christ, is not necessarily to do more, or to do spectacular things, but to act with an attitude of service. Then, what we do for our family will spill over outside our home to the people near us in our neighborhood, and in our community.

"A life that is not lived for others is not a life."
■ MOTHER TERESA[54]

Passing on the Faith

One of the most important services Catholic spouses are called to provide is to pass on their faith to their children and grand-children. Many parents feel at a loss at what to do and rely on Catholic education to fill in for their responsibility. That is admirable but not enough. Catholic education is intended to supplement what parents teach at home. Faith is learned in the home; it is learned in our "domestic church." We mentioned above that our role as parents is to be priests and teachers in our own "domestic church." There is an axiom that belongs to our Catholic tradition that says that the way we pray shapes what we believe.[55] When it comes to the liturgy of the Church, it is our prayer that expresses what we believe. The same applies to the liturgy of your home (your domestic church). It is through your family prayers, your home liturgy, that you express what you believe and pass on your faith to your children. How do you pray in your home?

A friend of ours, Mickey, told us of a ritual he had established in his home when his children were young. Each evening, when his children went to bed he blessed each of them individually and said a prayer with them. As the two sons became teenagers, they felt embarrassed by this ritual and asked their dad to stop. The father complied but continued praying for them. Years later as one of the sons, Jim, was leaving to serve in the Middle East, standing at the airport in the last moments before boarding the plane, he turned to his father and asked for his blessing. He remembered the power of that parental prayer. With his blessing Mickey taught his children of God's presence in their life. Today, Jim has a family of his own. He has adopted his father's ritual of blessing his children before bedtime.

Personal prayers such as prayers before meals, saying the Rosary, and praying at bedtime; or other devotions, such as novenas; and communal prayer, such as attending Mass, are all rituals that become foundations that anchor our children's faith. They will carry these with them for the rest of their life, even if they stop practicing.

Our Children Learn from Us

Our call to serve extends beyond our front door, and our children learn this from us. Consider the lessons you teach your children when you help people in your community as a member of the Knights of Columbus, or of the Women's Auxiliary, when you serve as a lector at Mass, teach religious education, and are involved in many other activities in your parish or civic organizations.

Look around your neighborhood. Is there anyone who may need your help? We know a family that each year at Thanksgiving makes it their family project to go to a homeless shelter and deliver and serve the Thanksgiving meal to those present. Sometimes serving our neighbors simply means encouraging and supporting those who do the right thing.

Good Job, Mom!

In 2014 Pope Francis, while speaking to a group of educators, pointed out that to educate our children today we need to reconstruct the village.[56] It used to be that bus drivers, teachers, and other parents supported us in our responsibility to form our children; however, today in our communities we tend to be isolated, and young parents are on their own.

One Sunday I (Teri) was standing in line at Walgreens, and there was a family at the checkout counter in front of me. They were all dressed up, so I assumed they had just returned from church. It appeared to me that their young son, a little boy, had stolen a small item and the mother was not leaving until he returned it and apologized to the clerk.

She looked at me and at the line forming behind me with embarrassment, but the son refused to apologize. When he realized they weren't leaving until he apologized, he returned the small object he had taken with an apology.

As I watched the drama unfold, I thought of Pope Francis and wondered what he would do if he had been standing there, witnessing this moment.

The family and I left the store at the same time. Once outside, and feeling empathy for that mom, I patted her on the back and said, "Good job, Mom!"

Love Expands

A couple's vocation to serve is a call to make their husband and wife "we" into a "we" that is a family.[57]

Do your remember your private conversations about having children and how many you wanted before your wedding? I remember Teri dreaming out loud that she wanted to have six children just like her mother, and I, coming from a family of three, was secretly hoping it would not be so, I would say, "let's start with one at a time."

On their wedding day all couples married in the Catholic Church promise to welcome children. Just before reciting the vows, the priest asks the couple: "Are you prepared to accept children lovingly from God and to bring them up according to the law of Christ and his Church?"

Serving God with the gift of our fertility is an important part of a couple's call to build up the Church and society. When God created Adam and Eve, he did not say to them: "Now go and have fun!" He did not create them just to be each other's companions. He created them to serve him by being fruitful, and by tending to his creation through their work. Having children is one of the purposes of marriage.[58]

The Gift of Life

We, as husband and wife, do not create life. According to our Catholic tradition, God is the creator of life, and fertility is his gift to us so that we can collaborate with him in that creation.

This fact is often forgotten in today's society, which encourages us to control our fertility at will. The most expedient way, we are told, is through means that temporarily suppress our fertility. The Catholic Church does not agree with this view of life.

Sexual intercourse is an intimate expression of love that bonds the spouses, and through it the couple places their fertility at the service of God. This is why Catholics believe that sexual intercourse should always be open to the creation of life. All of married life is at the service of God. The Catholic Church teaches that contraception is contrary to God's design for sexual intercourse.

This does not mean that Catholics cannot plan their families. The Church advises couples that it is their duty to be responsible parents and to plan births according to their means and conditions; they are, however, to do so according to God's design for procreation (*Humanae Vitae*, 10).

For many years, Catholic and non-Catholic couples alike have found a way to harmonize their lovemaking with their natural cycles of fertility and infertility designed by God. To try to conceive, they have intercourse during times of fertility, and to postpone conception they have intercourse during times of infertility. Doctors and specialists have created reliable methods that successfully help couples track their times of fertility and infertility. These methods are known under the umbrella name of Natural Family Planning (NFP).

Natural Family Planning

Teri and I began our marriage using Natural Family Planning and in so doing postponed pregnancy for over a year. We wanted time to get used to each other and to save some money. We continued using Natural Family Planning after our first daughter was born. Using NFP made us aware of our bodies' natural fertility cycles and increased our communication and intimacy. A few years later, during one of Teri's yearly doctor's visits, her doctor told her that, due to a possible fertility problem, if we wanted to have more children we should do so now. The words of the doctor were chilling and made us realize that the gift of fertility was not one that we could take for granted. In the same way that we had used Natural Family Planning to postpone pregnancy, we used it to achieve it again, and we had our second daughter. The circumstances made us appreciate even more the gift of our fruitfulness and the fact that our children are gifts from God.

A few years ago, Teri and I had the privilege of visiting with several married couples in the Nashville area to explore with them various aspects of married life. One of the topics we discussed was Natural Family Planning (NFP). Couples embracing NFP look at life and their fertility as a gift from God to be used to serve him. To these couples NFP becomes a way of life that helps them grow spiritually and as a couple.

Jenny, married nine years, told us: "When we had difficulty conceiving a second time, we looked to Natural Family Planning to help us. We were successful. We realized that Natural Family Planning was a very practical way to manage our fertility." Her husband, John, added: "Using NFP made us more aware of our bodies, our biological rhythms together. Most of all, it increased our intimacy."

Joe and Theresa, married nineteen years, told us that they did not start their marriage practicing Natural Family Planning, but gradually, realizing that birth control was not helping their relationship, they decided to learn the Couple to Couple NFP method. Theresa explained: "In practicing this method we learn to communicate better with each other and discovered that there are ways to be intimate that don't always have to involve having sex." Joe commented: "Practicing NFP showed me that, as a man, I have self control; and because of it I have a better relationship with my wife."

Mark, married three years, shared with us: "I was a convert to Catholicism and I had never heard of Natural Family Planning. I learned about it a few years ago when we attended a Theology of the Body conference. I was inspired when I learned that through NFP I can show respect for my wife and follow God's plan for marriage." Carol, his wife, added: "I feel blessed to know that my husband loves me enough to respect the natural cycle of my body. He realizes that he can express love to me in many different ways and is willing to go through the abstinence period because he understands that our relationship is not just sexual."

The sixth jar of love is an attitude of service. Through serving one another we express our love concretely. Jesus gave us his personal example of what serving means. If he can stoop down to wash his disciples' feet, we can do the same for one another and the people in our lives.

PRAYER

Jesus, our model of love, on the night before you died
you washed the feet of your apostles.
You call us to serve through the sacrament of matrimony.
Help us to follow your example.

We bring to you our jar of service and
ask you to fill our marriage
with a desire to care for others more than ourselves.

*Give us the grace to step outside our comfort zone
and serve our spouse and those whom you place in our path,
always aware that the love that we share is a gift from you.*

Amen.

Together recite the Hail Mary, the Memorare, and the Glory Be (these prayers can be found on pages 10–11).

PERSONAL/COUPLE REFLECTION

1. What thoughts cross your mind when your spouse says to you: "Can you help me with something?" Are they positive or negative thoughts?

2. The authors write that our marriage is not about us. Do you agree? What is your marriage about? What is your mission as a married couple?

3. List the ways in which you practice the works of mercy in your home. (See *Catechism*, 2447.)

4. Is there anyone in your neighborhood who needs your help or would welcome a kind word or a smile from you? Who is it?

5. What prayers do you say in your home? What do you and your children learn about God and the Church from the prayers you pray?

6. What would you say to God to thank him for the gift of your sexuality and fertility?

7. What do you know about Natural Family Planning?

GROUP SHARING

1. The authors write that our marriage is not about us. Do you agree? What is your marriage about? What is your mission as a married couple?

2. List the ways in which you are practicing the works of mercy in your home.

3. The *Catechism* teaches us that you and your spouse are priests, teachers, and leaders in your home. What does this mean to you?

4. How do you pray in your home? What do you and your children learn about God and the Church from the prayers you say?

5. Are there prayers and rituals learned in your childhood that you are practicing today?

6. What would you say to God to thank him for his gift of your sexuality and fertility?

7. What are some places in your town or city where you could learn one of the methods of Natural Family Planning? If you do not know, where might you go to find out?

ACTION

This week be intentional about serving your spouse and your family. Do it with a smile for the glory of God.

Conclusion

The Journey Continues

WE HOPE THAT READING SIX JARS OF LOVE HAS BEEN AN EFFECTIVE SPRINGBOARD FOR INTIMATE CONVERSATIONS WITH YOUR SPOUSE AND MOST OF ALL A TOOL FOR PERSONAL GROWTH in the six attitudes that foster spousal love: welcome, faithfulness, generosity, forgiveness, compassion, and service.

Growing in our ability to love requires intentionality and effort. Dr. William Doherty encourages couples not to let their marriage go into "autopilot." To avoid drifting, Dr. Doherty recommends that couples develop habits that are beneficial to the relationship. He calls these "rituals." Rituals in a marriage are activities that have a special meaning to both spouses and are repeated at regular intervals.

Rituals that can reinforce the attitudes we want to nurture in our marriage are:

- *Welcome*: Greet each other when leaving or returning home. Give each other a heartfelt kiss before going to bed and upon getting up. Psychologists recommend a kiss that is more than a peck—one that lasts a few seconds.

- *Faithfulness*: Hold hands in public as a sign of being intimately connected with each other. Schedule a regular date night, a time for fun together. Stay in touch with each other during the day.

- *Generosity*: Have a meal together daily or as often as possible. Establish a routine of eating together: a time when you expect to have a meal without interruptions for you and your family. Develop times during the day when electronic gadgets are set aside because your time together is more important. Go to Mass every week, and go together, if possible. If one of you is not Catholic consider how you will worship together, and where your family will worship when God blesses you with children.

- *Forgiveness*: Avoid criticism and sarcasm. Establish your own ritual for reconnecting after you have a disagreement or have hurt each other. Saying "I'm sorry" needs to be part of the ritual. Create rituals for celebrating the joy of your reconciliation.

- *Compassion*: Listen to your spouse vent his or her frustrations of the day without interrupting or trying to solve the problem. Establish ways you can give each other comfort, such as a back rub, a massage, or just holding each other. Find out what each prefers; then agree to do this regularly.

- *Service*: Help each other with daily tasks. Appreciate what each one of you is doing for the other and for the family, and remember to say "please" when you need a favor, and "thank you" when your spouse has done something for you.

To move forward on your journey of love you will need to make changes. However, many of us resist change. Most of us are fairly comfortable with the way we are, even if our behaviors cause us problems from time to time. Because of this we tend to postpone doing what is good for us.

If we truly want to make some changes, let's start by turning to Mary and Jesus. They can help us in our marriage, as they did at Cana. One of the most powerful sources of grace is available to us in the Eucharist. Through our participation in the Mass, Christ gives us the strength to overcome our natural aversion to change, and he guides us in crafting new ways of interacting that are beneficial to our marriage and our family. Make regular Mass attendance one of your weekly priorities.

Let us ask Mary to help us by interceding with her son, Jesus, as she did at Cana.

PRAYER

Mary, Blessed Mother of Jesus,
at the wedding of Cana you said to your Son, "They have no wine."
You recognized that the couple was in need
and asked for his help on their behalf.

We humbly ask for your intercession in the times when we fall short.
We too need Jesus to fill our marriage with the good wine
of welcome, faithfulness, generosity,
forgiveness, compassion, and service.

We ask this through your intercession so that
by the power of the Holy Spirit
our marriage is transformed to reflect the love of Christ
and in so doing gives glory to the Father.

Amen.

Endnotes

1   William J. Doherty, PhD: *Take Back Your Marriage*, The Guilford Press, New York, 2001, pp. 11-13.

2   John Gottman, PhD and Nan Silver: *The Seven Principles for Making Marriage Work*, Crown Publishers, New York, 1999, p. 23.

3   National Marriage Project, *When Baby Makes Three*, Charlottesville, Virginia, 2011, pp. 31-32.

4   Pope Francis, Festival of Families at Croke Park in Dublin, Ireland, August 15, 2018.

5   Pope Francis, homily at Santa Marta, December 18, 2013.

6   National Marriage Project, *When Baby Makes Three*, pp. 30-31; pp. 28-29. A study conducted in 2011 by the National Marriage Project at the University of Virginia found that among the top predictor of marital happiness for couples with young children is their spirituality: their faith practice, and the support of their community. The study reports that 64% of wives and 59% of husbands who attend church services regularly are "very happy" in their marriage. They also found that 82% of wives and 73% of husbands who have family and friends that support their marriage are "very happy."

7   Catholic News Agency, "Pope Francis: Think 'being good' is enough? It's not. Go to Mass." Collected 12/15/17: https://www.catholicnewsagency.com/news/pope-francis-think-being-good-is-enough-its-not-go-to-mass-22935.

8   Pope Francis, Angelus, October 29, 2017, "God, who is Love, created us to
    make us participants in his life, to be loved by him and to love him, and
    with him, to love all other people. This is God's 'dream' for mankind."
    http://w2.vatican.va/content/francesco/en/angelus/2017/documents/papa-
    francesco_angelus_20171029.html.

9   Pope Francis, *Evangelii Gaudium*, 7.

10 Pope Francis, Apostolic Exhortation *Amoris Laetitia*, 317.

11 Holy Mass for the opening of the Synod of Bishops, Homily, October
    7, 2012. Text found at http://w2.vatican.va/content/benedictxvi/en/
    homilies/2012/documents/hf_ben-xvi_hom_20121007_apertura-sinodo.
    html. Retrieved on 12-24-17.

12 Ashley McGuire, "Does the Family that Prays Together Really Stay
    Together?" Institute for Family Studies, April 20, 2016. Collected online
    on 8/3/18 at https://ifstudies.org/blog/does-the-family-that-prays-together-
    really-stay-together.

13 The State of Our Unions, Marriage in America, 2011: *When Baby Makes
    Three*. National Marriage Project, University of Virginia, December 2011,
    pp. 18-46, 30.

14 Jubilee Pilgrimage of his Holiness John Paul II to the Holy Land, homily,
    March 24, 2000. Text found at https://w2.vatican.va/content/john-paulii/
    en/travels/2000/documents/hf_jp-ii_hom_20000324_korazim-israel.html.
    Retrieved 12/24/17.

15 Pope Francis, Special Audience for Engaged Couples on St. Valentine's
    Day.

16 Pope Francis, Santa Marta homily, December 17, 2013, "This is holiness: to
    let God write our history."

17 St. John Paul II, *Letter to Families, Gratissimam Sanae*, 1994, Year of the
    Family, 15.

18 Pope Francis, Santa Marta homily, April 24, 2013.

19 Pope Francis, Apostolic Exhortation *Gaudete et Exultate*, 23-24, Rome, 3-19-2018.

20 St. John Paul II, *Letter to Families*, 19.

21 *The Rites of the Catholic Church*, Pueblo Publishing, New York, 1983. Rite of Baptism for One Child, p. 215.

22 *The Rites of the Catholic Church*, p. 223.

23 John Gottman, PhD and Nan Silver, *The Seven Principles for Making Marriage Work*, Crown Publishers Inc., New York, 1999, p. 100.

24 *The Seven Principles for Making Marriage Work*, p. 101.

25 Pope Francis, February 14, 2014, St. Valentine's day audience with engaged couples.

26 *The Seven Principles for Making Marriage Work*, pp. 176-177.

27 Pope Francis, *Amoris Laetitia* (*The Joy of Love*), 139.

28 *The Seven Principles for Making Marriage Work*, pp. 129-130.

29 *Marriage: Love and Life in the Divine Plan*, United States Conference of Catholic Bishops, Washington, DC, 2009, p. 33. "The Holy Spirit binds the spouses together through their exchange of promises in a bond of love and fidelity unto death. Their marriage covenant becomes a participation in the unbreakable covenant between Christ the Bridegroom and his Bride, the Church."

30 Wilder, Thornton, *The Skin of Our Teeth*, 1942.

31 *Marriage, Love and Life in the Divine Plan*, United States Catholic Bishops, Washington, 2009, p. 33. "Their marriage covenant becomes a participation in the unbreakable covenant between Christ the Bridegroom and his Bride, the Church."

32 *Marriage, Love and Life in the Divine Plan*, "authentic married love is caught up into divine love." p. 33.

33 Second Vatican Council, *Gaudium et Spes*, 48.

34 Pope Francis, Audience, February 12, 2014.

35 Benedict XVI, *God Is Love*, Ignatius Press, San Francisco, 2006, 6.

36 *God Is Love*, Ignatius Press, San Francisco, 2006, 6.

37 Jeffrey Dew, W. Bradford Wilcox, *Give and You Shall Receive? Generosity, Sacrifice and Marital Quality*, The National Marriage Project, University of Virginia, 2011, p. 5.

38 Michele Weiner Davis, *Divorce Busting* at http://www.divorcebusting. com/a_time_together.htm. Information collected 7/22/18.

39 W. Bradford Wilcox and Jeffrey Dew, The National Marriage Project, at the University of Virginia, 2012. Information collected June 6, 2018 at http://nationalmarriageproject.org/wp-content/uploads/2012/05/NMP-DateNight.pdf.

40 Anne Fishel, PhD. The Family Dinner Project, FAQ, collected on the Internet on 6/11/2018. https://thefamilydinnerproject.org/resources/faq/

41 Cody C. Delistraty, The Importance of Eating Together, Family dinners build relationships, and help kids to better in school, *The Atlantic*, July 18, 2014, collected on the Internet 6/11/18 at https://www.theatlantic.com/ health/archive/2014/07/the-importance-of-eating-together/374256/.

42 Dr. Dave Currie, Marriage: Are Electronic Devices Anti-Marriage? August 2016, collected June 22, 2018, http://www.doingfamilyright.com/ electronic-devices-anti-marriage/

43 Dr. Dave Currie, Marriage: Digital Delirium Part 2: Creating Wise Digital Boundaries, September 2016, http://www.doingfamilyright.com/marriage-digital-delirium-part-2-creating-wise-digital-boundaries/, collected June 22, 2018.

44 Jeffrey Dew and W. Bradford Wilcox, *Give and You Shall Receive? Generosity, Sacrifice and Marital Quality*, National Marriage Project, University of Virginia, 2011, p. 7.

45 John Gottman, PhD, *Why Marriages Succeed or Fail*, Simon and Schuster, New York, 1994, p. 68.

46 Abbott, *Documents of Vatican II*, The Pastoral Constitution on the Church in the Modern World, 48.

47 Linda J. Waite and Maggie Gallagher, *The Case for Marriage*, Doubleday, New York, 2000, p. 56.

48 Patricia Love, EdD, and Stephen Stosny, PhD, *How to Improve Your Marriage Without Talking About It*, Broadway Books, New York, 2007.

49 Pope Francis, tweet from World Youth Day, July 2013.

50 Tara Parker-Pope, *For Better: The Science of a Good Marriage*, Dutton, New York, 2010, pp. 99-100.

51 *Catechism of the Catholic Church* (CCC, 1535): Priests are consecrated to feed the Church by the words and grace of God. Spouses are consecrated to carry out their roles as spouses and parents. "Through these sacraments those already consecrated by Baptism and Confirmation for the common priesthood of all faithful can receive particular consecrations. Those who receive the sacrament of Holy Orders are consecrated in Christ's name 'to feed the Church by the word and grace of God.' On their part, 'Christian spouses are fortified and, as it were consecrated for the duties and dignity of their state by a special sacrament.'"

52 Dogmatic Constitution on the Church, *Lumen Gentium*, November 21, 1964, 11: "The family is, so to speak, the domestic church. In it parents should, by their word and example, be the first preachers of the faith to their children; they should encourage them in the vocation which is proper to each of them, fostering with special care vocation to a sacred state."

53 *Lumen Gentium*, November 21, 1964, 31: "The faithful who by Baptism are incorporated into Christ, are placed in the People of God, and in their own way share the priestly, prophetic and kingly office of Christ, and to the best of their ability carry on the mission of the whole Christian people in the Church and in the world."

54 Mother Teresa, sourced from World Quotes, http://www.worldquotes.in/
mother-teresa-quotes, 9/29/18.

55 *Lex orandi, lex credendi* is an axiom passed on through the centuries in the
Church and explained in the *Catechism of the Catholic Church* as follows:
"The law of prayer is the law of faith: the Church believes as she prays"
(CCC, 1124).

56 Pope Francis, Address of Pope Francis to Participants in the International
Meeting of Directors of "*Scholas Occurrentes*," Rome, September 4, 2014.

57 John Paul II, *Letter to Families*, 16: "In rearing children, the 'we' of the
parents, of husband and wife, develops into the 'we' of the family, which is
grafted on to earlier generations, and is open to gradual expansion."

58 *Marriage: Love and Life in the Divine Plan*, Pastoral Letter of the United
States Conference of Catholic Bishops, Washington, DC, 2009, p. 11):
"Marriage has two fundamental ends and purposes toward which it is
oriented, namely, the good of the spouses as well as the procreation of
children."

ALSO AVAILABLE

Happy Together
The Catholic Blueprint for a Loving Marriage

This comprehensive resource identifies and focuses on six key aspects of a loving marriage and uses stories and examples to illustrate each. Recommended for married couples, engaged couples, and marriage enrichment groups.

168 PAGES | $16.95 | 6" X 9" | 9781585956852

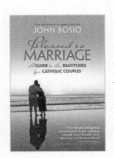

Blessed Is Marriage
A Guide to the Beatitudes for Catholic Couples

John Bosio draws from his experience as a family therapist and committed believer to provide a path for a loving marriage inspired by the Beatitudes. He offers couples both theological grounding and inspiration as they seek to strengthen their marriage commitment.

104 PAGES | $14.95 | 6" X 9" | 9781585958566

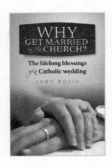

Why Get Married in the Church?
The Lifelong Blessings of a Catholic Wedding

This warm and welcoming booklet invites engaged couples to discover the grace, mystery, strength, and wonder of the Catholic sacrament of marriage and provides honest answers to commonly asked questions.

24 PAGES | $1.95* | 5½" X 8½" | 9781585959075
bulk pricing is available

TO ORDER CALL 1-800-321-0411
OR VISIT WWW.TWENTYTHIRDPUBLICATIONS.COM

TWENTY-THIRD PUBLICATIONS
A division of Bayard, Inc.